INSTITUTE OF LEADERSHIP & MANAGEMENT

SUPERSERIES

Organizational Culture and Context

FOURTH EDITION

Pergamon
Flexible
Learning

Published for the
Institute of Leadership & Management by

OXFORD   AMSTERDAM   BOSTON   LONDON   NEW YORK   PARIS
SAN DIEGO   SAN FRANCISCO   SINGAPORE   SYDNEY   TOKYO

Pergamon Flexible Learning
An imprint of Elsevier
Linacre House, Jordan Hill, Oxford OX2 8DP
30 Corporate Drive, Burlington, MA 01803

First published 1986
Second edition 1991
Third edition 1997
Fourth edition 2003
Reprinted 2004, 2005, 2006

British Library Cataloguing in Publication Data
A catalogue record for this book is available from the British Library

ISBN 0 7506 5884 3

For information on Pergamon Flexible Learning
visit our website at www.bh.com/pergamonfl

Institute of Leadership & Management
Registered office
1 Giltspur Street
London
EC1A 9DD
Telephone 020 7294 3053
www.i-l-m.com
ILM is a subsidiary of the City & Guilds Group

Working together to grow
libraries in developing countries

www.elsevier.com | www.bookaid.org | www.sabre.org

ELSEVIER   BOOK AID
             International   Sabre Foundation

Authors: Colin Everson with additional material by David Pardey
Editor: Jane Edmonds
Editorial management: Genesys, www.genesys-consultants.com
Composition by Genesis Typesetting, Rochester, Kent
Printed and bound in China

Contents

Contents

Workbook introduction

1 ILM Super Series study links

This workbook addresses the issues of *Organizational Culture and Context*. Should you wish to extend your study to other Super Series workbooks covering related or different subject areas, you will find a comprehensive list at the back of this book.

2 Links to ILM Qualifications

This workbook relates to the following learning outcomes in segments from the ILM Level 3 Introductory Certificate in First Line Management and the Level 3 Certificate in First Line Management.

C3.1   Organizational context
1. Recognize the value of an organization for achieving objectives
2. Identify alternative forms for an organization's legal entity
3. Describe the range of functions necessary to maintain an effective organization
4. Identify effective organization structures
5. State the typical roles and responsibilities of managers at different levels of the organization
6. Identify stakeholders in own organization

C3.5 Organizational culture

1 Understand organizational cultures and their impact upon managers

2 Identify and describe the dominant culture within own organization and the management styles which embody that culture

3 Understand the impact of 'sub-cultures' within teams and departments

4 Appreciate the value of empowerment, delegation and leadership in managing the team sub-culture

C3.7 Ethics in business

1 Understand the concept of ethics and its relevance for the workplace

2 Identify and resolve situations where individuals may have different perceptions and apply different values

3 Identify and resolve circumstances where individual and organizational value systems may be in conflict

4 State the measures that an organization currently takes to demonstrate acceptance of social responsibility

5 Understand ways in which organizations communicate ethical values

3 Links to S/NVQs in Management

This workbook relates to the following elements of the Management Standards which are used in S/NVQs in Management, as well as a range of other S/NVQs.

C4.1 Gain the trust and support of colleagues and team members

C4.2 Gain the trust and support of your manager

C4.3 Minimize conflict in your team

It will also help you to develop the following Personal Competences:

■ acting assertively;
■ behaving ethically;
■ building teams;
■ managing self.

4 Workbook objectives

All of us deal with organizations large and small every day of the year. One organization collects the rubbish regularly, another supplies water, another runs the shops and others provide the daily necessities of life. Organizations educate children, care for the sick, serve charitable causes, and provide entertainment, car servicing, public transport, and the goods and services that people expect to be available in a modern society.

Unless you live on a desert island, you simply cannot get away from organizations.

Most of the people reading this book work for an organization in the public or private sector of the United Kingdom's massive economy. This is presided over, to some degree, by a government which itself is a massive organization.

How do, or should, organizational structures differ?

But are all organizations much the same? Should they all have the same basic structures? Or are there different kinds of organization that are best suited to achieving particular objectives? For example, is a structure designed to generate and distribute electricity also suited to achieving the aims of a charity or to developing new 'high tec' products in the IT field?

Have ethics and moral values any role to play in commercial business?

It is evident that religious bodies, public organizations established to provide healthcare programmes, or private charities established to help particular groups should have some ethical basis.

But what about the private, commercial sector? Is making money the only valid objective, or should account be taken of wider community issues, even in areas where the law does not specifically require it? Can 'good' ethics also be 'good business'? Is there something other than short-term profit, or increases in share price, that matters, even though it doesn't show immediately in the profit and loss account or the balance sheet?

Organizational culture and internal politics

Is there such a thing as culture in an organizational sense? If so, do some cultural stances encourage most people to do their best, most of the time – and others have the opposite effect?

And what is it within an organization that can prevent it from achieving its objectives, even if these are clearly defined and appropriate, and the 'right' organizational structure appears to be in place? Can there be factors operating against the organization's aims from within, sapping its strength, just as a tapeworm does when it grows inside the human intestines?

These are all questions that this book will ask you to face. It will encourage you to continue to examine them in every aspect of your life, at work and in organizations that you deal with in any capacity outside work.

In Session A, we will focus on the reasons for having organizations, the varied legal structures which they use, what makes them effective – or not – and why the modern economy could not continue without them.

In Session B, the spotlight falls on the ethical and moral aspects of organizations in every sphere of activity. We will examine just what is meant by ethics in the organizational sense and the conflict that can exist between individuals' ethical standards and those of the organization for whom they work.

In Session C, the question of organizational culture and internal politics will come under the microscope. Organizations vary widely in their management styles, and in the extent to which they are successful in taking the majority of their staff with them along the path which they have chosen. The way in which the aims of individuals, or groups of individuals, may conflict with, or even undermine, those of the organization will be analysed.

4.1 Objectives

When you have completed this workbook, you will be better able to:

- understand the value of an organization to achieving objectives, and the power of an organization to act by comparison with non-organized action;
- describe the forms that organizations can take, the functions required to maintain them, and the proper roles of managers at various levels within them;
- distinguish between different organizational structures and their 'fitness for purpose' in differing situations;
- recognize the importance of organizational and business ethics in general and their application to your own workplace;

- understand the concept of stakeholders and identify the stakeholders in your organization;
- appreciate the conflicts that can exist between individuals' values and those of the organization for which they work;
- appreciate the range of organizational cultures that may exist and recognize their specific effect on your own workplace;
- recognize the value of delegated authority and be ready to use it within your own working environment.

5 Activity Planner

You may decide to look at the following activities now, so that you can start collecting materials in advance of tackling them

Some or all of these activities may provide the basis of evidence for your S/NVQ portfolio. All Portfolio activities and Work-based assignments are sign posted with this icon.

Activity 14, on page 27 asks you to describe the organization that you work for and the various links you have both within it and with any external organizations. You may find it helpful to obtain a copy of your organization's own Organization Charts as a basis for your answer.

Activity 21, on pages 45–6 requires you either to:

- identify the designated stakeholders in your own organization from existing documents;
- or suggest who the principal ones should be, if such policies do not yet exist.

Activity 24, on pages 52–3 asks you to obtain a copy of your organization's mission statement and produce a short assessment of its impact on the day-to-day running of the organization. If such a statement doesn't exist, you are asked to suggest how the example provided in Extension 2 might be adapted.

Activity 26, on pages 60–1 asks you to obtain a copy of your organization's annual report and/or related documents and gather selected information from them. If your organization does not publish any equivalent documents, a list of organizations from which you can obtain them is given in Extension 3.

x

Activity 28, on pages 65–6 requires you to identify the means by which you can raise sensitive issues in your organization, while Activity 39, on page 96 asks you to consider the nature of your organization's culture and sub-cultures.

Session A
Why organizations need to exist

1 Introduction

'They couldn't organize a booze-up in a brewery' is typical of the derogatory comments that are made frequently about unsuccessful activity in every walk of life – from sport to politics, and from high-level business to the local horticultural society or social club.

The signs of disorganization are easy enough to recognize – people rushing around, often working very hard individually, but achieving little collectively.

If, then, the signs of disorganization are obvious to anyone, what should you observe when an organization is 'well run'?

Activity 1

2 mins

From your own experience as a customer, as a user of public services, entertainment and sport, jot down as many signs as you can that an organization is working *smoothly*.

_____

_____

_____

Your answers probably all said in effect that, when an organization works smoothly, you hardly notice it is there at all. For example:

- the corps de ballet dance in unison, the players in an orchestra play their assigned parts in tune and on the beat, and the actors in a stage play know their lines and speak them 'in turn' as written by the author;
- the players in a football, hockey, basketball or netball team seem to know 'instinctively' where the ball should be despatched to next;
- the shelves of the local shop are stocked with all the 'best-selling items', and the mail order company delivers your order on time and in good condition;
- a fire engine arrives promptly in response to a '999' call and the crew know where the hydrants are, how to use the equipment and get on with the job, with little need for the officer in charge to say anything.

EXTENSION I
Extension I examines briefly the organizations of a computer and a living being.

People often use phrases like 'running on oiled wheels' to describe the tangible effects of good organization. In Extension I you will find examples of two kinds of organization that it is easy to take for granted as they generally work so smoothly.

But, as you will know from experience, good organization in the managerial context does not just happen. It involves a great deal of hard work 'behind the scenes'.

All the above examples of good organization involve teams of people working towards a common purpose. The individuals within these teams may or may not be well organized on a personal level. However, if they are well organized, their collective talents, experience and goodwill can be wasted by a badly structured organization, or a well structured one that is badly run.

2 What organizations are for

If any organization is to be worth having, then the result it achieves should be such that:

'the whole is greater than the sum of its parts'.

It is not uncommon to find that sporting teams whose individual players are not 'stars' perform better than teams containing a number – perhaps even a majority – of 'big names' .

Activity 2

2 mins

Can you suggest some **organizational** reasons for:

- a superior performance from a team of 'moderate' individuals;
- a disappointing performance from a team that includes many 'stars.'

_____

_____

_____

> The Tour de France bicycle race is one of the most gruelling of all sports. The prestige of winning it is incalculable. The successful teams tend to be those which designate one member as their preferred winner and organize the team to do everything they legitimately can to help him win. This means that, from the outset, most of the team know that they cannot win – though their legs will ache just as much or more – but that overall they are organized to give the team its best chance of success.

You may well have suggested something along the lines that:

- the moderate performers are willing to combine themselves into a team and are committed to the joint objective of defeating the opposition;
- they recognize each others' strengths and weaknesses;
- they co-operate by playing to those strengths and compensating for the weaknesses;
- they listen to the team manager and team captain with respect;
- they feel they should do their best where they are, as there is no 'queue' of other clubs waiting to sign them up.

Conversely:

- some of the 'stars' may be more concerned with their individual performance than with the result achieved by the team;
- they may be less willing to listen to the team manager and captain;
- they may even wish to prevent other individuals from 'shining' too brightly if this may detract from their own 'brilliance';
- they can always go elsewhere if this team doesn't produce the success they deserve.

In the first case, the organization produces a result where the 'whole is greater than the sum of its parts'. In contrast, the star-studded team produces a result well below its combined potential.

Of course, there are no hard and fast rules in management, and there are many star performers who have the humility and good sense to subordinate their own aims and egos to a common purpose. It depends on:

- how worthwhile the organization's purpose is perceived to be by the majority of its staff;

■ how well its structure is designed to accommodate the team members and individual talents they possess;

■ how well it is managed at every level.

All three elements need to be present for any organization to function well. They are like the legs of a three-legged stool. Remove any one of the legs and the stool will collapse under its own weight, before any external pressure is applied.

3 Is there an 'organization for all purposes'?

'Organization' is used in common speech as though it has a single meaning, but is that true? Is there a single organizational structure which will work for all purposes?

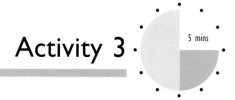

Activity 3 · 5 mins

Imagine you are asked to set up a number of organizations to achieve the following purposes:

■ to buy specialist goods from North Africa and the Middle East and sell them entirely via the Internet;

■ to raise money for a charity via a chain of shops, 90% of whose workers will be unpaid;

■ to organize a celebration for the 50th anniversary of the local tennis club;

■ to supply electricity to the whole of a UK region, comprising 20,000 square miles, 2 million households, plus a mix of large industrial and commercial users;

■ to research into finding improved methods of treating a rare debilitating disease.

What differences, if any, do you think there should be between the structures of the organizations you set up? Jot down your ideas.

_____

_____

_____

_____

_____

_____

Compare your own thoughts with the following about suitable structures to serve these widely differing purposes.

■ An organization buying goods from a number of countries, and selling them on the Internet, would require a network of contacts in the countries involved, some of them fluent in the languages spoken. It would also require expertise in designing and operating web sites and ensuring that everyone gets paid. It would need to be flexible, to cope with varying supply and demand for the products.

■ Managing mainly unpaid volunteers requires a very different approach to, for example, the structure that would work for a commercial retailer. Lines of communication need to be kept short and the volunteers must be chosen for their commitment to the charity's purpose and reminded constantly _why_ they subscribe to it.

■ For a 'one-off' purpose, such as organizing a celebration, the need is for an informal group of self-motivated people who are committed to the task and can bring different skills and experience to bear upon it – for example, one who is familiar with the club's history, another who can publicise the event and help put that history into pictures and words, another who can deal with raising and accounting for any money required and another with expertise and/or contacts in catering. All must be prepared to work without pay and discipline themselves to attend meetings and carry out the tasks which they agree to undertake with minimal – or no – supervision.

■ A massive undertaking, such as supplying electricity to a whole UK region, has huge safety health and social implications. It requires a formal structure, staffed by competent specialists who react to virtually any circumstance – from bad weather to terrorism – and develop tremendous technical and administrative expertise.

■ Intensive research would demand the use of original thinkers and highly individual experts, who would almost certainly resent the rigid structure required to supply electricity. Some of them might need to be paid more highly than managers more senior to them in the organization in 'hierarchical' terms, to attract the calibre of specialist required.

The workable organizational structures that have evolved over the centuries have taken their basic **purpose** as their starting point. Where problems arise it is because:

- the organization's purpose is ill-defined, or has changed over time;
- a structure inappropriate to the purpose has been imposed;
- the people who work in the organization have not been convinced that they should support the organization's purpose, and/or resent a structure that they find either too rigid or too unsupportive.

Various combinations of these ills are possible, and ailing organizations frequently suffer from all three.

The Millennium Dome was built on reclaimed industrial land with some £0.5 billion capital funding from the National Lottery. The New Millennium Experience Company (NMEC), which built it, was a public company with a single share owned by a Minister, initially Peter Mandelson and subsequently Lord Falconer. Its Board was chaired by Bob Ayling (of British Airways) and contained politicians, business people and figures from the arts and entertainment industries. Its first chief executive, Jennie Page, was seconded from the Civil Service but she resigned halfway through the year because of the financial difficulties NMEC faced. Her replacement (Frenchman Pierre Yves Gerbeau) was recruited from Disneyland Paris.

The Dome was part of a wider economic development on the Greenwich peninsular, including new housing and improved transport infrastructure. The major problem for the Dome was that it was never quite clear whether it was educational or for entertainment – a science and culture exhibition or a theme park, reflecting the fundamentally Christian nature of the millennium or the multi-faith nature of the UK today. To complicate matters further, the high profile involvement of a government meant that it took on a highly symbolic status, so that its success or failure was seen by many government critics as indicative of its general competence.

Added to this, according to a National Audit Office report, the Millennium Dome was badly managed, its visitor number target of 12m was 'ambitious and inherently risky' and it was 'clear that the task of managing the project had been complicated by the complex organisational arrangements put in place from the outset, and by the failure to put in sufficiently robust financial management'. The NMEC had 'weaknesses in financial management and control' and it had been unable to 'track and quantify fully the contractual commitments it has entered into'. The company 'experienced difficulty in establishing the full extent of its liabilities through to solvent liquidation and handover to a new owner'.

In response to these comments, Lord Falconer said: '... we should not lose sight of what has been achieved. The dome is the number one pay-to-visit attraction in the UK, with over 5.4m visits so far – with visitor satisfaction ratings among the industry's highest'.

Activity 4

Think back to the three-legged stool and describe briefly where you see signs of potential failure with any of its legs in the case of the Millennium Dome.

■ Purpose

_____

_____

■ Appropriate structure

_____

_____

_____

■ Managerial competence

_____

_____

_____

You almost certainly identified cracks in all three 'legs'.

■ **Purpose**
It was very unclear what the Millennium Dome's main purpose was. Was it an engine of economic and social development on the Greenwich peninsular, or was the site chosen for political reasons? Was it to attract overseas visitors, or was it primarily for UK citizens? Was it to inform or entertain?

■ **Structure**
The Dome was a complicated operation, requiring large numbers of people, first to build it and then to operate it. The management of a construction business is always going to be different from that of a 'visitor attraction' and this inevitably put pressure on its organizational ability. According to the NAO its 'complex organisational arrangements' suggest that it was poorly

The Millennium Dome closed at the end of the year 2000, and has remained empty and unused at the time of writing. Its continuing embarrassment to the government emphasizes the failure to be clear about the long-term as well as the short-term purpose of the building.

structured to achieve its purpose – whatever that was! Furthermore, the politicized nature of the Dome, its mixture of Board members from business, arts, entertainment and politics, was always likely to lead to conflicts.

■ **Managerial competence**

The NAO were highly critical of the management of the Dome with criticisms of its 'failure to put in sufficiently robust financial management' and 'weaknesses in financial management and control', its inability 'to track and quantify fully (its) contractual commitments' and its 'difficulty in establishing the full extent of its liabilities'. A civil servant, however competent, is unlikely to have the experience needed to run a large-scale public attraction, and the fact that her replacement was recruited from Eurodisney suggests that this was recognized, but too late to overcome all the problems.

The importance of purpose, structure and managerial competence

This example of the Millennium Dome has shown that the three-legged stool view of an organization works even for the most complex examples. The problems faced by Equitable Life and Marconi in the UK, and Enron, WorldCom and Global Crossing in the USA at the beginning of the 21st century have certainly proved this to be the case. Failure can stare any organization in the face if it does not:

■ define a clear purpose;
■ establish a structure appropriate to achieving that purpose;
■ manage at every level to gain continuing commitment from the vast majority of staff for most of the time.

Communication is at the heart of the third leg of the stool and is fundamental to managerial competence at all levels. A manager's job is to get things done through other people, however large the organization may be.

4 Types of organization

Many types of organization have developed over the centuries, ranging from the sole trader, through partnerships in which a number of people pool their resources and expertise, to private or public limited companies, with tens or thousands of shareholders. There are also organizations, such as co-operative societies and trades unions, which have evolved to give their members collective strength to counterbalance that of organizations with whom they must negotiate or compete. And there are charities, some of them very large organizations employing many paid staff as well as volunteers.

We have looked at the different requirements made on organizations by different purposes and the way in which their structure needs to reflect their purpose. Many legal requirements are placed on organizations too, as you will see in this section.

4.1 The sole trader

Sole traders, in particular, are responsible for many inventions and innovations. If you work for an oil refining company and design a new form of engine which doesn't use petrol, you may not be too popular – think of all the 'vested interest' they have in petrol refining, amounting to billions of £'s. But, as an individual, you might be able to sell such an idea to a large company which does not have an interest in suppressing it.

The vast majority of businesses in the UK are small, with more than 80% employing fewer than ten people. A large proportion of these are in the sole trader category.

This is the simplest form of business to run, from an organizational and internal communications point of view, as it is typically a self-employed person. Motivation is provided automatically for most by the basic need to earn a living in the absence of a regular wage or salary.

However, there are many pressures on the sole trader, whatever trade or profession is being pursued.

Activity 5

From your own experience, list some examples of 'sole traders' with whom you have dealt:

- in trades, such as shopkeepers or window cleaning;
- in professions, such as dentistry or general practice as a doctor.

_____

_____

_____

_____

- List any pressures you think any sole trader might be under, in what you consider to be the order of significance.

_____

_____

_____

The examples of sole traders are so many and various that your list could contain any number of examples, from fishmongers to soul singers and shoemakers to authors. A comparative list is given on page 123.

As far as the pressures go, these are common to all of them. You have probably listed many of the following, even if you haven't put them in the same order.

- Staying healthy – illness is a constant anxiety for anyone 'going it alone'.
- Deciding what business is 'right for you'.
- Getting business from credit worthy customers.
- Meeting the quality standards of customers.
- Getting paid in reasonable time.
- Providing money for working capital, capital investment and the future.
- Accounting for the monies received and paid.
- Keeping up to date with the law and their own speciality.
- Using time effectively.

The list of broad categories shows that the sole trader has to look after most of the functions which the largest 'mega corporation' has. He or she must also do it without the help of specialist managers found in large organizations unless, of course, they:

- buy services in from accountants, lawyers, marketing or other specialists;
- join a trade association or federation that can provide them with back-up services as part of the membership package, for which they pay an annual fee.

The sole trader does not have to manage internal human resources', but must:

- deal effectively with people who are customers, suppliers and employees of official bodies;
- if wise, practise rigorous 'self appraisal' on every aspect of personal performance.

Most attention in the media is focused on the very largest organizations in the public and private sectors. However, much of the dynamism and original thinking that a country needs are generated by sole traders and small businesses. They are free of the shackles of vested interests, hierarchies and rigid reporting relationships, all of which often smother new ideas in large organizations.

The government and other organizations are increasingly recognizing the importance of small organizations to the UK,

The Confederation of British Industry (CBI), though associated in most people's minds with 'big business', has an Enterprise Group devoted to furthering the interests of smaller businesses. It acts both to influence the UK government and the European Union (EU).

In 2002, the Labour government stated that it wished to become the party of the small business and the self-employed as well as of employees.

Unlimited liability

Undoubtedly, the threat to a sole trader's personal assets is one of the greatest sources of anxiety. The law provides protection for the shareholders of incorporated private and public companies through limited liability (which

The consequences of unlimited liability are shown by what happened to many 'names' in the Lloyds Insurance business, following several years of disasters in the 1990s. Many of the largest risks were insured by Lloyds and they called upon the 'names' or members to pay. At the time, it was a condition that the names accepted unlimited personal liability. Many lost virtually everything they possessed, amounting to hundreds of thousands of £s or more.

we will discuss in section 4.4). However, the law does not allow a sole trader to register as a limited liability company. And even if it did, many businesses would undoubtedly demand personal guarantees, secured on the trader's private property – typically a house – before agreeing to give them medium- or long-term credit in the form of, for example, bank loans or overdrafts.

If large customers are slow to pay, or don't pay at all through insolvency or fraud, then the sole trader can be placed in a desperate financial position. Lloyds members (see the margin box) are not alone in facing financial disaster. Many a sole trader, in sport, entertainment, commerce and industry, has lost everything after a seemingly glittering career. Often, it is through unwise speculation, poor financial management – or the attentions of 'fair-weather friends' who melted away at the first signs of chill winds blowing away the fortune that they had been helping to 'manage'.

Until limited liability companies were recognized by the law (in the mid-nineteenth century), the threat to individuals' personal assets was a real barrier to enterprise. The threat was there for both sole traders and partners in an unincorporated partnership.

4.2 Partnerships

There are many practical advantages to taking the step from being a sole trader to becoming a member of a partnership.

Activity 6 · 3 mins

What advantages should a partnership business have over that of a sole trader? Jot down at least four.

_____

_____

_____

Your list of advantages could have included:

- having more capital available to invest without borrowing and paying interest to a bank or other third party;
- having a wider range of skills and contacts available;
- avoiding the need to employ expensive specialists (e.g. in accountancy, information technology, marketing) to do jobs which various partners can undertake;
- having more chance to manage time effectively and spread the administrative burden involved in running any business;
- having opportunities to discuss and resolve immediate problems, including competitors' activities, with a sympathetic group of people;
- having the chance to generate new ideas through discussions and brainstorming sessions;
- having the facility to review performance in every aspect of the business and look for continuous improvement;
- having someone to take over if a key partner is away on holiday, ill, or in any other way unable to give the business their full attention for an extended period of time.

Surely the main advantage is that you no longer have to be a 'one-person band'.

Each can focus on what they are good at if, say:

- one partner can produce wonderful ideas which work, but is naturally shy;
- another is an extrovert who loves dealing with customers;
- and another understands financial matters.

Of course, they still need to agree on the three broad issues:

- What the organization is setting out to do.
- What structure will be used to ensure effort is not duplicated and what responsibility and authority each partner has.
- How the business will be managed at each level, to ensure that everyone – including employees who are not partners – remain committed to its purpose.

Equal or unequal partners?

Members of partnerships are often equal partners, sharing the risks, responsibilities and rewards equally. However, the partnership deed, under which the partnership is registered legally can apportion all of these matters in any way that the partners agree upon. Some may take a much more active role than others and be rewarded accordingly.

There may be 'sleeping partners', who provide capital and share in any profits made, but take no active part in the day-to-day running of the business.

In *Animal Farm*, George Orwell's 1940s allegorical tale on the move to the totalitarian organization of society, the pigs gain the upper hand. They declare that 'all the animals are equal, but some are more equal than others' – a mathematical impossibility but a reality in many societies – and partnerships.

Many partnerships are relatively small, close-knit operations – often in professions such as the law, accountancy, or property services operating locally. But you may have come across some which have many, even hundreds, of partners, such as some of the national and international partnerships in law, property, accountancy and management consultancy.

In practice, the very large firms have moved right away from the original idea of a few people sharing their expertise and financial resources. They must operate just like any other large organization.

Some of the partners are 'more equal than the others'.

Can you imagine a committee of hundreds of equal partners reaching a decision about anything in a reasonable time?

Disadvantages of partnerships

One disadvantage that all partners share with sole traders is that of unlimited liability. This can be a real disincentive to borrowing money from outside the partnership. But it is not the only, or indeed the chief, reason why so many partnerships fail and often end up in acrimonious court proceedings.

Activity 7 · 2 mins

Can you suggest three or four factors that may undermine partnerships which, if not addressed, can lead them to be dissolved?

_____

_____

_____

You probably listed factors, including the jealousies and clashes of personality that beset any group of equals working under pressure. 'I do all the work, but they're getting as much as I am' is a common complaint. Simple dishonesty, where one partner absconds with partnership funds, or employs 'friends' at inflated prices to act as sub-contractors, is another. Spouses, relatives and friends may be given partnership roles on the basis of friendship rather than business acumen or saleable skills.

A whole series of TV programmes has focused on the stresses that arise when groups of individuals are put together in demanding situations with no defined leader. At its worst, a partnership may exhibit the same destructive tendencies.

The business may grow beyond the level at which some partners are competent to manage – but the agreement may still provide that partner with a right to take decisions that the others cannot challenge.

Succession can be a real problem if a partner retires, decides to pursue another career or has an accident. The partnership really exists only as the sum of the skills and experience that individual partners bring to it. Its effectiveness can quickly decline if one or more of the key people leave, or become less effective, for any reason.

Of course, many partnerships survive for decades or longer, well beyond the working lives of the original partners. This is because they have found a way of organizing their affairs to ensure that the 'three-legged stool' remains stable, that is:

- they continue to have a clear purpose, adapted to suit changes in the requirements of customers and clients;
- their organizational structure is well-defined;
- the partners who manage the entity are competent leaders, who communicate effectively and continue to motivate their fellow partners and employees.

Partnerships really can have advantages over the sole trader. It is significant that they so often involve people in professions that do not need to raise large amounts of finance for premises or capital equipment.

4.3 Franchise organizations

Before moving on to limited companies, franchising is worth examining. Businesses ranging from the sole trader to large public companies use it as a way to get started or to expand. Under a franchise agreement, the franchisor (often a very large organization) allows the franchisee (usually, but not invariably, a much smaller organization) the exclusive use of a famous brand name like McDonalds, BMW, Prontaprint, or Spar in a defined territory, which may be a town, a district within a large city, or a larger geographical area, depending on the size of the potential market.

In return, the franchisee usually agrees to:

- pay an 'entry fee' ;
- sell solely or mainly the franchisor's goods;
- buy from nominated suppliers;
- uphold quality standards so as not to bring the brand 'into disrepute';
- set prices and mount promotional activity according to plans agreed with the franchisor;

- usually provide any necessary premises and/or vehicles;
- possibly make regular payments for continuing support.

Franchising is now such a common way of running a business that whole business conferences, magazines and departments of large banks are devoted to it. Some national newspapers devote regular space to it, as well as advertisements from prospective franchisors. The activities covered range from mobile dog washes to TV stations, and from bread, milk and frozen food delivery rounds to fast food restaurants, petrol stations and hotels.

Activity 8

3 mins

Can you think of some possible benefits of a franchised operation from the perspectives of:

- the franchisee;
- the franchisor?

Jot down two or three for each.

_____

_____

_____

_____

From the franchisee's perspective, the advantages should include:

- exclusive rights to sell a famous brand in a defined territory;
- access to marketing support, including advertising and structured promotional activity;
- quality-assured supplies of raw materials and reliable distribution services;
- professional training and instructional materials and services;
- continuing development of products and services based on the franchisor's market research and technical expertise.

From the franchisor's viewpoint, the advantages should include:

- rapid expansion into new areas without the need for heavy capital expenditure and complex project management;

- simplified, cheaper management, as the franchisee will take full responsibility for the new profit centre and has every incentive to make it succeed;
- higher sales volume against which to charge marketing expenses, providing a more economic unit cost;
- further, rapid market penetration and support for the brand.

The benefits

If you happen to work for a franchised organization, you will be in a strong position to assess the overall benefits to your employer. The chief benefit to a prospective franchisee is the strength of the brand that they will have the right to use, and the scale of the marketing budget that the franchisor will commit to support it. Campaigns involving TV advertising and structured promotional activity are way beyond the means of local entrepreneurs, but are the lifeblood of national and international businesses such as Kentucky Fried Chicken or Volkswagen.

Setting up 'Ken and Michelle's hamburgers' in your local town may not have quite the same impact as opening a new Wendy's or Burger King – however good your products and service may be.

The costs of obtaining a franchise and providing the premises, vehicles and equipment to operate it can be very high. Consequently, many of the more expensive franchises are actually operated by large limited companies, who have more money and credit available.

Expensive is a relative term. Remember:

- the cost of the franchise should be related to the risks and benefits associated with it and the potential returns on available capital;
- the 'packages' offered by the large operators may look expensive, but their 'street cred' with customers and their expertise in marketing may well produce higher sales and a better return than a cheaper franchise.

Barrier to entry

This is a phrase worth keeping in mind, especially if you ever think of starting your own business, franchised or otherwise. The following example illustrates this piece of management or economist's jargon.

After working for some years as a manager in a food-processing business, Sheila Stockton decided to set up her own business providing high-quality home-made pickles, sold entirely via the Internet. She organized suppliers throughout the local market gardening area in which she lived and invested in a web site through which to market them. She also managed to gain publicity for her new venture via a number of specialist magazines and some of the more general lifestyle titles, leading to an appearance on a BBC programme. She sank a great deal of her savings into the venture and virtually 100% of her waking hours for several months, as well as taking out a substantial loan on the basis of her business plan.

Sales grew steadily over the first few months and seemed to be justifying the risks she had taken in leaving a good job. Then, the sales figures first plateaued and then fell alarmingly.

A search of the web revealed that three other suppliers had started up since she had begun, and all were undercutting her prices significantly.

Sheila could not afford to cut prices, because of the interest she had to pay. Then, one or two of her suppliers reneged on their contracts, pleading that they had been made offers by her competitors which 'they couldn't afford to refuse'. This peak Christmas season came and went without significant improvement to the figures.

Sheila was suffering from the classic symptoms of a low 'barrier to entry'. The business she had gone into required little capital resources and was technically quite simple to run. She had spent heavily on promotion and, ironically, by doing so had helped expand a market into which it was easy for others to follow her. Her products had no edge in quality over the competitors – they were exactly the same – nor could she offer quicker delivery. So, why should her customers pay more for the same product and service?

There was a relatively low 'barrier to entry' for her competitors – financially, technically and organizationally – and before long her business folded, leaving her with shattered dreams and significant debts.

This sad story has been reproduced many times in many kinds of small businesses through the ages. Among the more recent examples was the collapse of the many service-orientated 'dot com' companies.

Of course, there are many businesses that have very high barriers to entry. For example:

- steel making requires enormous capital investment and technical expertise;
- operating a postal service like the Royal Mail is incredibly complex logistically, as well as requiring vast amounts of capital resources;
- establishing a plant nursery requires great horticultural skill and expertise, retailing acumen and considerable working capital reserves to care for plants while they are growing, sometimes over several years, before they can be sold.

It is when there *is* a high barrier to entry such as these that the limited company comes into its own.

4.4 Limited companies

Together with the public sector corporations, limited liability companies are the largest organizations in the UK economy. There are equivalent organizations in every developed country, with a similar legal status and operating in similar fashion. Because people hold individual shares, or 'bundles' of shares called stocks, such companies are often referred to as 'joint stock' companies.

So, what is the significance of the 'Ltd' abbreviation, or the letters 'plc' after the name of a large organization like Boots, Halifax, or Corus? In law, it is a very significant one. Any company incorporated under the Companies Act and registered by the Registrar of Companies at Companies House is regarded as having a distinct personality. The incorporated company assumes an identity legally separate from that of the directors and managers who run it.

The limited company can:

- make contracts, or be sued, in its own name;
- be prosecuted under the criminal laws and Acts of Parliament, such as the Health and Safety at Work Act;
- has liability limited to the value of its issued share capital.

After the scandal of the 'South Sea Bubble' in the early eighteenth century, successive British governments were wary of allowing the formation of any joint stock companies, seeing them as providing opportunities for wholesale fraud and deception. However, as the industrial revolution proceeded, private individuals found it difficult to raise large sums of capital. They were unwilling to risk their entire fortunes in sole trader enterprises. Eventually, the joint stock company was rehabilitated, by a series of Acts of Parliament that began in 1844.

There have since been so many Acts and amendments, and the Law is now so complicated, that many lawyers do nothing but work in this area. Numerous textbooks are devoted to the topic. Here we will focus on the broad principles, particularly:

- the consequences of limited liability;
- the ability of limited liability companies to raise large sums of capital;
- the way in which an organization with a 'fictitious personality' must be managed.

Limited liability

This protection for the shareholders of a company grants them great peace of mind. In essence, the law says that there can be no greater demand made upon shareholders than the value of the shares they have agreed to buy.

Activity 9

Michael agreed to subscribe to a share offer made by a limited company. He bought 1,000 shares in a company for £7.50 per share. He was to pay £2.50 per share initially, and two further instalments of £2.50 when 'called' for by the company. He paid the second instalment, or 'call', after 18 months. Three months later, the company went into liquidation and his shares became effectively worthless.

- The company's debts amounted to £10,000,000.
- There were 1,000 shareholders.
- So the average 'debt per shareholder' was £10,000,000/1,000 = £10,000.

What was Michael's actual maximum liability for the company's debts?

Under the law, Michael was only liable to pay the balance remaining on the shares he had agreed to buy – that is, £2,500. This represented just one quarter of the amount that averaging the company's debts over the total number of shareholders would produce. Of course, he had also lost £5,000 through paying the first two calls. But contrast his situation with that of the unhappy Lloyds' names referred to earlier.

Protection for creditors and 'third parties' generally

Much of company law is aimed at protecting those who deal with limited companies, including their employees, from dishonest company managers. This can give an observer a negative view of limited liability companies, not improved by the accounting scandals of their US counterparts in the early twenty-first century.

> If all people acted honestly, there would be little need for any criminal or statute law at all. Laws are inevitably made to protect society from the dishonest minority – and the Companies Act is no exception

However, in practice the vast majority of companies run their affairs honestly and it is generally thought that accounting standards required in the UK are significantly higher than those in the USA. The advantages to the total UK economy of raising capital for large-scale businesses, which would otherwise not exist, far outweigh the disadvantages and problems caused by a small number of unscrupulous operators.

In some circumstances, the courts can 'lift the veil' of incorporation, in the graphic phrase used by the lawyers. Where there is evidence of wrongdoing, such as trading while the directors know a company does not have enough money to cover its liabilities, the courts can proceed directly against the assets of company directors who have acted in ways that prejudice the interests of third parties.

Raising capital

Whereas a private limited company has a legal upper limit placed on the number of its shareholders and cannot sell shares to the general public, the public limited company (plc) has no such limitations. It can therefore raise large amounts of capital both from individuals and from other companies.

If you think about a business venture requiring £25 million to establish itself, the arithmetic shows clearly how powerful an organization the 'plc' is for raising capital.

■ A sole trader would have to use his or her own resources, or borrow from banks on the security of their own fortune. Few people would be able *and* willing to raise £25 million in this way.
■ A partnership is in a better position, but if there were 25 partners, they would need to raise £1 million each and would still have 'unlimited liability'.
■ A private limited company with 50 shareholders, would have to demand an average of £0.5 million from each of them (though at least their liability would be limited).
■ *But* a 'plc' could sell shares to any number of investors. If sold to 10,000 people, their average liability would be limited to £2,500 – a much more reasonable sum.

This example explains clearly why the 'plc' is able to raise such enormous sums fairly simply, subject to many legal safeguards as to what the company is allowed to do with the money. It explains why virtually all the largest companies in the UK are 'plc's, though there are some very large private limited companies, usually still mainly under the control of the family which founded the business.

Managing an organization with a separate legal identity

Though an incorporated company has its own legal personality, it cannot actually do anything without human intervention. That, coupled with limited liability, has caused the law to prescribe:

■ that a company may only legally do what the 'memorandum of association' (filed prior to registration) sets out as its purpose;
■ how, in general terms, the company must manage its affairs, as set out in its 'Articles of Association' (also part of the registration process).

The memorandum of association

Think back to the 'three-legged stool' for a moment. In essence, the memorandum sets out the *purpose* of the company that forms its first leg. It cannot do anything else without going through a legal process to amend its

The Rover company originally made bicycles, towards the end of the nineteenth century. If its memorandum of association had stated that the sole purpose of the company was to manufacture and sell bicycles, it would have been unable to diversify into motor cars some years later, unless it went through a tedious legal process.

memorandum. This is completely different from a sole trader or partnership, which can choose to do anything it wishes to, at any time – provided of course that it is itself legal.

This provision can be very limiting on a plc's activities. Though it is often obvious what a company intends to do to earn a living, it is not always so. And companies often need to change over the years, as the markets that they serve change.

Company directors now draw up their memoranda in very broad terms, enabling them to change and diversify without the need for amendment.

Activity 10 · 2 mins

Suggest how the memorandum of association could be worded to allow the Rover Company to diversify from manufacturing bicycles to manufacturing motor cars, filling in the gaps in this sentence.

'The purpose of this Company is to manufacture, distribute and sell _____ form of _____ for use by individuals or public service operators.'

You will find a suggestion in the Answers to Activities on page 123. It may differ from your own, but the basic point is that by saying they were in the transport business, or words to that effect, the company gives itself room to manufacture anything from a pogo stick to a motor coach, an aircraft or an ocean liner.

Many companies developed into conglomerates in the twentieth century, involving themselves in an extremely wide range of activities.

There are fashions in business, as well as on the catwalk. Conglomerates are now out of fashion and Tomkins has sold many of its businesses – including both the 'guns and buns' makers.

The multi-billion £ turnover Tomkins plc company became known as the 'guns to buns' company in the City of London, during the 1990s because it ran businesses that included gun manufacture (in the USA) lawnmowers, plumbing supplies, rubber components for cars and aircraft, windscreen wiper blades, birthday cakes (for Marks & Spencer) gravy browning, bread, frozen meat pies – and yes, buns.

You would never have guessed this from the simple name Tomkins. On the other hand, it's apparent that the former British Steel Corporation' (now part of Corus) was likely to be involved in steel making.

Copies of both the memorandum and articles of association are public documents, which anyone can inspect through Companies House. It's worth doing if you have any concerns about dealing with a company, to assure yourself about exactly what the company is able to do legally.

The articles of association

These, for a limited company, provide the second leg of the stool, setting out its permanent organizational structure. The articles specify:

- how directors are to be appointed and what authority they have;
- how powers are to be allocated between the directors and the shareholders.

These articles cannot be changed without the agreement of shareholders, another safeguard for investors.

The 'directing mind'

Despite these legal safeguards, it can still be difficult to know who is really responsible for a company's actions. The larger the organization, the farther is the 'man or woman at the top' from its activities at grass-roots level.

If you think back to the sole trader, there is no problem in deciding who made a decision over any aspect of the business. But when it comes to a huge plc employing tens of thousands, at hundreds of sites, every second of the year, it becomes a very different matter.

Many vast organizations are clearly identified with a particular person. Bill Gates, the founder of Microsoft – one of the world's largest organizations – is clearly identified with it. Richard Branson is likewise identified with Virgin and all the businesses it operates.

What the law tries to do, however vast an organization may be, is identify a senior figure as the 'directing mind'. This person can be held accountable for an event, wherever and whenever it happened. It may involve finance, safety, product quality, environmental health – indeed anything that concerns those who deal with an organization or work for it. Even in the largest company, there must be someone who is ultimately responsible, just as there is in the very smallest 'sole trader' business.

4.5 Public sector, voluntary sector and 'self help' organizations

So far in this book we have dealt chiefly with organizations in the private sector, which usually have to make a profit to survive. However, there is an enormous public sector which provides many essential services to the community.

Activity 11

List up to six organizations that operate in the public sector, either by type or by quoting specific examples in your own area.

_____

_____

_____

What do you think is one **major** difference between private companies and public sector organizations?

_____

_____

You will find a list of organizations that operate in the public sector in the Answers to Activities on page 124.

Profit centre vs. Cost centre

The major difference between private companies and public sector organizations is that, broadly speaking, private organizations are **profit** centres. They must make a profit to survive, whereas public sector bodies are **cost** centres, which must aim to control their spending within allocated budgets. They do not usually have to make a surplus, or profit, to fund new investment.

Nevertheless, the three-legged stool model applies just as well to public sector organizations as to any other. They must:

■ be clear what their purpose is;
■ have an appropriate organizational structure;
■ manage their employees at all levels to retain their commitment.

Public sector organizations are answerable to local or central government and through them to the electorate. The electors have the ultimate say as to whether their objectives are the right ones and whether they are being achieved at an acceptable cost.

The voluntary sector

Private charity is an honourable and long established aspect of British life. Visit any town or city and you will probably find almshouses, often endowed by benefactors hundreds of years ago, but still carrying out the original purpose of their founders. Since these founders are long dead, they must have established a structure, in the form of a charitable trust, to ensure that their intentions would continue to be carried out. There are many larger charities whose names are household words, again many of them long-established and still basically doing what their founders intended them to do.

A formal legal process must be followed to establish a charity. The body set up to vet and oversee their establishment and subsequent activities is the Charity Commission, which is approximately equivalent to the Registrar of Companies.

The purpose of a charity

As with a limited company, the purpose must be clearly stated in the registration document and in practice, will be more narrowly focused than that of most limited companies. It would be difficult or impossible to register a charity with very far-reaching aims.

Imagine a charity that supported vivisection for medical research on the one hand and opposed all cruelty to animals on the other. These are mutually incompatible and there would probably be very few donors to the charity.

> Charities including the RSPCA and its Scottish equivalent, the NSPCC, Barnardo's, Oxfam, the Cheshire Homes and St. John's Ambulance, control substantial funds. Much of their income is in the form of legacies that the donor entrusts them with after his or her death.

Activity 12

A charity was registered with the object of ' improving the lot of working horses in the Indian sub continent'. Some years later, a request was received from a field worker in India for funds to mitigate the plight of mules and donkeys working in an industrial brickfield near New Delhi.

- Could the charity legally help?   YES/NO
- If not, what would it need to do so that it could?

_____

_____

_____

The charity would have been unable to help as things stood legally. Although donkeys and mules are related species, they are *not* horses and its objective was helping horses. It would need to amend its purpose, with the consent of its supporters, to read more generally. If it substituted the word 'equines' for horses, then horses, donkeys, zebras and any other equine species could be helped legally.

Because charities are entrusted with large sums of money, often in cash, the rules governing how they must operate and what they are allowed to do with the money have to be very strict. Charities do enormous good with the money they receive in the UK and throughout the world.

Charities *have* to be above suspicion, or their funding will reduce and they will be much less able to serve the causes they were established to help.

In the case of all the organizations described, there are specific legal requirements as to registration and the ways in which they must be run to retain their status and legal recognition.

Other organizations with roots in charity and 'self help'

In this session we've looked at several important types of organization, but there are still many more.

Activity 13 · 2 mins

What types of organization have not yet been described in this session but are important in UK Society? List three or four significant ones.

_____

_____

_____

You may well have suggested any of the items in the list given in the Answers to Activities on page 124. Those which continue to have a significant effect on the UK's economy and social fabric are described below.

■ **Trades unions**
Workers began to organise themselves to counterbalance the power of their employers. Though the focus of unions has changed, they remain important organizations, which depend on a great deal of voluntary work at the shop (or office) floor level. They provide a wide range of welfare services to members

as well as negotiating payment and conditions of work with their employers. They have also been heavily involved with Health and Safety legislation, which has helped improved the conditions of work for everyone.

■ **Co-operative societies**

Co-operative societies are immensely important commercially, and collectively they figure amongst the UK's largest retailing organizations. They retain close affinity to their roots in the industrial towns of the nineteenth century and take a strong ethical stance over many issues concerning the UK and countries in the developing world. Some directors may be elected to the board from amongst employees and society members. There is a strong emphasis on supporting local communities.

■ **Building societies**

Many have now changed their status and become plcs. However, there are a significant number of societies registered under specific building societies legislation, which allows them less commercial freedom. They contend that they can offer a better and more economical service to their members by retaining their original status.

■ **Mutual and friendly societies**

These organizations were closely related to insurance companies. They provided very inexpensive policies to help poorer people to 'help themselves', particularly against sickness, old age and funeral expenses. Many of their functions have now been taken over by the state, or are provided for in other ways. Originally, they demonstrated yet another way in which people could organise themselves, even in adverse circumstances, and produce a result whose sum was 'greater than the sum of its parts'.

'Form should follow function' is a well-recognized principle of architecture. It stands to reason that a castle should have a different structure from a hotel, a school from a prison and a domestic house from a hotel.

We've seen that the many ways in which people can organize themselves are reflected in the different types of organization. They are also reflected in the range of structures that organizations adopt, a subject to which we turn in the next section.

5 Organizational structures

'Structure' includes the allocation of formal responsibilities, the typical organization chart. It also covers the linking mechanisms between the roles . . .'

Charles Handy *Understanding Organizations*

Activity 14

20 mins

S/NVQ C4.2

This Activity may provide the basis of appropriate evidence for your S/NVQ portfolio. If you are intending to take this course of action, it might be better to write your answers on separate sheets of paper.

Describe the organizational structure within which you work, including all the respective job titles involved. Use charts and diagrams wherever they will help to show clearly where you fit in – and try to include all the important informal links you have. If official organization charts are available, modify these to show the real situation as you see it.

On your charts show all of the following links (except where they don't apply to you), plus any others you can think of.

a   Direct reporting relationships

- who works directly for you;
- who works directly for them and so on;
- to whom you report;
- to whom that person reports and so on through to the senior manager.

b   Indirect/informal reporting relationships

Who you deal with in other departments – or other sites – within your organization:

- on the same level as yourself;
- more senior to yourself;
- junior to yourself;
- in specialist departments, e.g. safety/technical/human resources/mainten-ance/cleaning.

c   Links to other organizations

What frequent contacts you have with:

- customers;
- suppliers;
- external advisers, trade associations;
- official bodies – such as Environmental Health, Building Control, Health & Safety Executive: Trading Standards.

There will be as many different answers to this activity as there are readers of this workbook. You may not have been able to show links to all the people and organizations listed above, for example, you may never have direct contact with your organization's customers. On the other hand, you may have identified links not included in the list.

Charts are a very useful means to describe organizations. They will be used in this section to help explore the strengths and weaknesses of different types.

5.1 Hierarchical structures

Roles within a hierarchy

Organizations are often shown as a triangle.

- The Managing Director or Chief Executive at the apex at the top.
- Then a board of directors, each taking responsibility for a defined function, such as Finance.
- At the next level, departmental managers who report to the functional director: in Finance, these might comprise information technology, accounting, payroll, data protection.
- Then first line managers who report to each departmental manager: in accounting they might look after accounts payable, accounts receivable, credit control and bank transactions.
- Finally, at the base, the operators who do the routine work, which would be clerical staff in the case of the Finance Department.

Responsibilities at different levels

The job titles and number of layers will vary with the size and type of organization. But there are factors that all hierarchies have in common.

- In general terms, the closer a manager is to the apex of the triangle, the less he or she should be involved with day-to-day routine. The Managing Director should be concerned predominately with long-term strategy, with looking at external influences on the organization; with judging its strengths, its weaknesses, the opportunities which it should grasp and the threats it must counter.
- The nearer to the base that a manager operates, the more he or she must be concerned with ensuring that the daily routines of selling, manufacturing, distributing and accounting for earned and spent money operate efficiently.
- The roles are mutually dependent – there's no point having a marvellous strategic thinker as Managing Director if the business is haemorrhaging money on a daily basis. Conversely, first line managers will be wasting their time and energies controlling day-to-day affairs if the company is heading in the wrong direction for the medium or long term.
- The nearer to the apex you get, the less obvious it becomes what you *should* be doing.

Many senior managers find it very hard to think about the long term and immerse themselves in the detail of day-to-day activity because they wish to be busy and earn their salaries. Nearer to the base level, managers and staff can become disillusioned and disaffected if there is constant interference, or if the organization's purpose is not clear to them and they are unsure about just what they are meant to be doing.

Why have so many layers and functions?

Reverting to the sole trader for a moment, role and responsibility are clear-cut and there is no complex structure to get in the way. All the functions are in the trader's own hands. But large organizations need to have defined responsibilities and lines of communication if they are to run smoothly: there isn't time for one manager to look after several complicated functions. It's also impossible for everyone to talk to everyone else, or for decisions to be made by committees involving everyone in an organisation that employs hundreds or thousands of people.

A typical hierarchy

The diagram below shows a typical hierarchical structure for a large organization, with several tiers of management between the most senior and least senior members. If the structure is adhered to rigidly, then there will be no contact directly between the different 'lines', such as F-E-D-C-B-A and F-G-H-I-J-K.

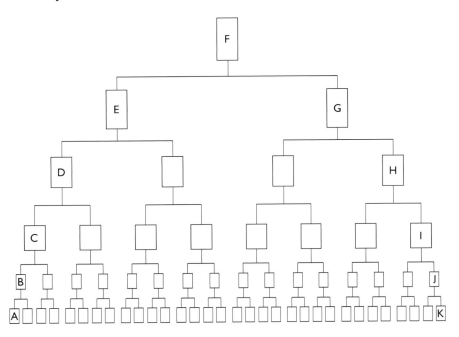

Such structures have been traditional in the armed services, the police, in large engineering companies and effectively in multi-site operations – retailing, catering and distribution. Each of the blocks across from level C might represent a local depot manager with two supervisors reporting to him.

Activity 15

What do you think are:

- the advantages of such a structure:
- the disadvantages?

Relate your answers to your own experiences, with present or previous employers and with other organizations you have deal with.

_____

_____

_____

_____

Advantages of hierarchical structures could include the following.

- Everyone knows where they stand, who reports to them and to whom they report. If the structure is implemented logically, people at every level will know exactly what the limits of their authority are.
- There is an identifiable promotional path from level A to level F, though there are obviously many fewer jobs at the higher levels.
- In the military sphere, if someone is killed or incapacitated in battle, succession is automatic on the basis of rank (and seniority, for example, if the brigadier at level D is killed and there are two colonels at Level C in the diagram, then the Colonel who had been promoted to that rank first would take over).

The disadvantages could include the following.

- The rigidity of the structure can encourage lack of initiative and a 'jobsworth' attitude.
- Communication can be very slow between the different 'lines'. For example, what happens if the manager at any level is away?
- Where quick reactions are required 'on the ground', the people best able to take the decision may be forbidden to do so until the message has gone up to level F and come all the way back down again. By that time, it may be too late.

In practice, relationships between people in different lines will almost always develop for any number of reasons. If, for example, your brother or someone you were at school with, works in another department, will you really never use that link to 'get things done' outside the formal structure? Or if you are a local manager with initiative and integrity, will you always wait for a remote senior manager to tell you how to do your job?

A young management services manager was assigned to a project in Nigeria, where her organization had a depot in Lagos. On the third day of her project, the local General Manager, George Deauville, said 'Oh, by the way, Nicky, I've arranged for us to go up to Ibadan to look at the depot there this weekend.'

'How long have we had a depot there? They didn't mention it to me back in London,' replied Nicky, puzzled.

'That's because I haven't told them yet,' replied Deauville. 'I was sure there was a good opportunity there – it's one of the largest cities in Africa.'

'But what happens if it fails?' persisted Nicky.

'It won't. But, if it should, then I'll close it or sell it – and no one at Head Office will be any the wiser, unless you tell them. Would you?'

Nicky smiled and shook her head.

This true story shows that people 'on the spot' with initiative, local knowledge and spirit will usually find ways of overcoming the more restrictive aspects of a hierarchy, even if they aren't several thousand miles away from 'head office'

5.2 The 'wheel'

The next diagram is of another structure with which you may be familiar. It shows ten team members revolving around one designated chief decision maker. All the team members really are equal and all may talk to each other if they wish to.

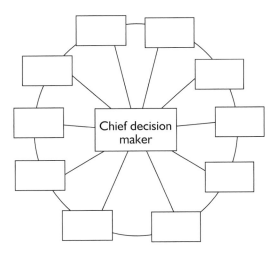

Activity 16

4 mins

Again, referring to your own experiences where possible, note down what you believe to be:

■ the advantages of this management structure;

■ its disadvantages.

_____

_____

_____

_____

_____

_____

> The founders of Tesco, Marks and Spencer and the Burton tailoring group all remained at the hub of their businesses for many years after they had become substantial businesses, far removed from their basic origins as small-scale retailers and tailors.

The fact that everyone is able to talk to each other has some advantages. But it can also have drawbacks in that, since nobody but the person at the centre of the wheel can take decisions, the other ten people may become little more than a 'talking shop'.

The decision maker, of course, should know very quickly what is going on and be able to respond swiftly to changing circumstances. But, what happens if he or she is away for any reason ? Or lacks the expertise and insight to weigh up the situation correctly and so makes a wrong decision?

Though this structure is typical of smaller companies, it is not that uncommon to find large organizations, even governments, that revolve entirely around one central decision taker, most often to their detriment.

The transition from a 'small' business, where such a structure can be successful, to a larger one that is usually beyond the capacity of one person to keep a grasp on, is one of the most difficult to make. Many fall by the wayside, or sell out to larger organizations that have the organizational expertise to cope with the complexities and sheer volumes of data generated by large-scale activity in the public, private or voluntary sectors.

5.3 Flat management structure

Many companies have tried to delayer their hierarchies and remove tiers of management – and cost – in the process. A structure that has been subject to this approach is shown in this diagram.

Activity 17

3 mins

■ What conditions do you think must be met if a 'flat' management structure is to work successfully?

_____

_____

■ For what overall *purposes* might it be the ideal choice?

_____

_____

The designated team leaders must have sufficient delegated authority for such an organization to work. They must also have the expertise and self-confidence to run their affairs without constant reference to their 'boss' for guidance and support.

Organizations that are bad at delegating authority will struggle if this structure is imposed, and the team leader's authority and self confidence will be constantly undermined.

Opportunities for promotion are likely to be few in a 'delayered' hierarchy, which can demotivate ambitious people.

A flat organization is ideally suited to the purpose of growing a number of 'sub-organizations' quickly in parallel. A charity, for example, that wishes to expand rapidly, might do so, using dedicated people in the team leader role. They may be volunteers with no wish for promotion.

If you have worked for an organization which has stripped away layers of management, you will have your own experience and opinions as to its advantages and potential pitfalls.

5.4 Functional management structure

The three forms of organizational structure that we've looked at so far have something in common: they provide a designated leader at some point. But is this always necessary?

The functional management structure says there doesn't have to be one leader.

The next diagram shows such a structure, under which the line managers report separately to whichever function is involved with their current activity. For a new product launch, that might be the group marketing manager; for a new engineering project it might be the group engineering controller and so on. The site may or may not have a designated 'general manager'.

FUNCTIONAL MANAGEMENT STRUCTURE

Note: Chart shows situation when four projects are happening together, a normal situation for a large organization to be in

Activity 18 · 3 mins

- This is a quite different approach to structuring organizations. Like the others we have looked at, it has its strengths and weaknesses. What do you think they are?

- Can you suggest an overall organizational purpose that it is well suited to?

The advantages to the line manager may be that he or she has constant access to genuine expertise and to senior managers able to provide support.

Against that, the line manager can suffer the classic dilemma of serving two (if not several) masters, some of whose demands are conflicting, all of whom are senior in rank and between whom he or she cannot arbitrate. In addition, they have no responsibility for general site issues, such as employee relations, security, health, safety, cleaning, general maintenance and relationships with the local community.

The site manager, if there is one, loses much authority to people beyond his or her control and yet retains responsibility for anything that is done which may prejudice the general standards of management. If there is *no* site manager, then who takes responsibility for all the general matters?

Like the other structures, the functional structure has a place, possibly in an organization directed towards marketing or design-led activities.

5.5 What are the objects of organizational structures?

In the descriptions of organizational structures, words like 'up'; 'down'; 'more senior' and so on are used, implying that some staff are 'more equal than others'. That is evidently true, in terms of the rewards which people tend to receive as they progress 'up' through an organization. But:

- should a management structure be built upon the shoulders of the people who drive the buses, staff the charity shops, teach the children, deliver the mail – in fact do any of the countless jobs usually shown at the bottom of the chart?
- or should the structure exist to underpin their activities, requiring managers to bear those for whom they take responsibility upon *their* shoulders?

Particularly if you have been promoted from the shop floor, you will probably have your own views on this.

> A major manufacturing group faced a national strike. Management and supervisory staff were not involved and nor were some shop floor employees. Many sites were able to carry on limited production.
>
> It was immediately apparent that the key activity was packaging, involving fearsomely complicated machines, many of which appeared to have 'minds of their own'. An impromptu management structure was soon evolved in which it was recognized that the key 'managers' were:
>
> - experienced supervisors, engineers and operatives who understood these machines and could operate and maintain them.
>
> The more senior managers' role became one of supporting their junior colleagues by:
>
> - ensuring that supplies of raw materials and packaging continued to arrive in the right amounts;
> - servicing the packaging machine operators by physically moving the stocks of finished products and packaging materials to them.
>
> Much of the work that senior managers did would have been considered unskilled labour, and they took instruction from the junior colleagues who were much 'closer to the action' than they were.

The BBC ran a series of TV programmes called 'Back to the floor' in which senior managers, in widely differing businesses, worked alongside their shop floor colleagues. Though they did not do so 'incognito', their common experience was that too often their people and the FLMs (first line managers) who managed them were *imposed upon*, rather than *supported by* the organizations for whom they worked.

This example is not intended to demean the role of senior managers under normal circumstances, when they should properly be concerned with medium to longer-term issues. It simply underlines that:

- structures need to be designed to suit the purpose that the organization is seeking to achieve, in this case keeping the business going;
- the aim of management should be to reduce the burden on those who do the work that earns the organization its living;

■ it is no bad thing for managers at every level to find out just how much they depend on the people who are so often spoken of in the media as being at the shop floor level.

5.6 Reorganization

Writing around AD 60, Petronius Arbiter said: 'I was to learn later in life that we tend to meet any new situation by re-organizing. What a wonderful method it can be for creating the illusion of progress whilst producing confusion, inefficiency and demoralization.'

Depending on whom you have worked for, you will have experienced re-organization more or less frequently. The quotation from Petronius Arbiter is close to 2,000 years old, but may well raise a wry smile from you.

Many organizations in the public, private and voluntary sectors seem to re-organize with astounding frequency, often producing confusion, inefficiency and demoralization.

Even seemingly 'minor' changes, like moving the number of accounting periods in a year from calendar months to 13 '4-week periods' can cause confusion. The ability to compare like with like disappears and managers waste time reconciling figures and arguing about whether this year is really worse, or better, than last.

More major changes, like changes from a hierarchical or wheel structure, can have effects which last for years. In the worst cases, they can divert attention from the real purpose of the organization, whether it be public service, charitable or making continuing profits to assure the survival of the business. Large organizations frequently carry special provisions on their annual accounts for the costs of re-organization (or restructuring).

In principle, *evolution* is better than *revolution* when it comes to changing organizational structures.

All senior managers would do well to keep in mind the accounting maxim that 'no profits are generated *inside* a business, only costs.'

Though voluntary and public sector organizations are normally cost centres, rather than profit centres, they are still subject to this same financial 'law'.

■ The more they spend on internal matters, including reorganization, the harder it will be to manage within their budget . . .
■ and the less will be available for public service or charitable works.

6 Organizational functions

We've considered the difficulty that a sole trader has in being 'all things to all persons'. In larger organizations, the problem is overcome by employing specialists in various fields. The result is the typical organization chart shown here.

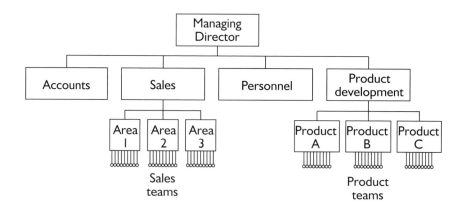

The context within which all organizations must work is now so complex that it would be impossible for the larger ones to survive without access to specialists.

■ Employment law alone can be a 'minefield' for organizations in the public, private and voluntary sectors. Thousands, or even millions of £s can be at stake if sound policies do not exist, or are not implemented.

■ Inexpert management of building and construction projects can bankrupt even a large company, or result in it being prosecuted by the Health and Safety Executive or the Environment Agency for breaches of the law.

Though specialist managers bring many benefits to an organization, they can also create problems of their own.

Activity 19

5 mins

List up to ten specialist functions that a medium- to large-scale organization needs to run effectively.

_____

_____

_____

_____

■ What might be the problems of integrating them?

_____

_____

■ How, in principle, do you think these problems might be overcome?

_____

_____

You will find a suggested range of functions in the Answers to Activities on page 124.

The heads of specialist functions will take a professional pride in their expertise and could be thought of as similar to the 'stars' in a sports team, or the principals in an orchestra.

Each will probably 'fight their corner', believing the discipline they represent to be the most important to the organization's well being. Up to a point, that is healthy, but it can lead to problems if all or some of them pull in different directions.

In principle, it is for the organization's general manager, managing director, chief executive (however the office is designated) to:

■ instil in the specialists respect for its overall *purpose*;
■ provide a structure that gives recognition to their expertise;
■ manage and communicate with them to maintain their commitment to the purpose;
■ ensure that, overall, the total of their contributions is greater than the sum of its parts.

This last point must be the objective of organizations in every sphere of human activity; otherwise there is no point in having them

■ Achieve this objective and the organization will be effective – but virtually invisible.

Self-assessment 1

20 mins

1 Complete this sentence.

The sign of a _____ organization is that the _____ is _____ than the sum of its parts.

2 Which of the following is the basis for continuing success in any successful organization in the long term? Underline your choice.

power/success/sound financial management/
excellent management communications/marketing

3 Put a tick against the correct answer.

Investing in a company's shares removes from investors the threat of

■ business failure;
■ unlimited personal liability;
■ take over by a larger business;
■ poor management decisions.

4 Suggest two disadvantages that partnerships share with sole traders.

_____

_____

_____

5 Why is becoming a franchisee now so popular as a way of starting, or expanding, a business?

_____

_____

_____

6   There are two kinds of limited liability company. What are they known as and what is the main difference between them, so far as raising money is concerned?

_____

_____

_____

7   Complete the following sentence.

Neither limited companies, nor registered charities, can do anything legally

other than _____

_____

8   Complete the following sentence.

One of the principal differences between a public sector and a private sector

organization is that the former is a _____ whereas the latter is

a _____

9   Fill in the blanks in the following sentence.

When considering a major _____ of their _____,

senior managers should bear in mind the maxim that 'no _____

is generated inside a _____, only _____'.

Answers to these questions can be found on page 121.

7 Summary

- It is easier to see the signs of **poor** organization than of good organization – but the latter takes great effort behind the scenes to achieve.

- All organizations which succeed in the longer term must have:

  - a clear **purpose;**
  - a **structure** designed to suit that purpose;
  - excellent and continuing **management communications** at all levels to retain the commitment of all employees to the organization's purpose.

- The main types of organization are:

  - sole traders;
  - partnerships;
  - franchise organizations;
  - limited companies;
  - public sector, voluntary sector and 'self help' organizations.

- More than 80% of United Kingdom businesses employ ten people or less, and many of the new jobs and new ideas in the economy are generated by small businesses.

- Most large private sector businesses are limited companies that, legally speaking, have personalities distinct from that of their directors and members. They can, for example, make contracts, or be sued and prosecuted in their own name.

- It is as inexcusable for public and voluntary sector organizations to be inefficient as for a 'profit making' concern. Inefficiency reduces the amounts they can spend on public services and charitable purposes.

- There is no single organizational structure which is suitable for use in every circumstance. The main structures are:

  - hierarchical;
  - the wheel;
  - flat;
  - functional.

- As organizations grow, it becomes impossible for one person to carry out all the functions required and it is necessary to employ specialists in areas such as engineering, marketing, personnel and finance. Managing the specialists effectively then becomes a major part of senior management's role.

- The task of managers at every level, whatever their job title, is to provide support to the people who report to them and not to impose unnecessary administrative burdens on them.

Session B
Ethics in business

1 Introduction

Dictionaries typically define ethics as:

> 'doctrine which deals with human duties and obligations. A code of morality'
>
> *King's English Dictionary*

In medicine, a more specific definition is usually given:

> 'conforming to a recognised standard in relation both to those who practise the profession of medicine and the medicines which they use.'
>
> *King's English Dictionary*

In the organizational context, the second definition may be more familiar than the first. Modern organizations are used to working to standards for quality, the environment, safety, food hygiene and customer service. Some do so willingly; some because it has been imposed by customers or government agencies.

Where duties and obligations are imposed by Government in the form of Statute Law, in areas such as Health and Safety and conditions of employment, a business has no choice but to observe them, as no individual or organization is above the law.

It is plain to see that ethical standards have a place in medicine generally and in religious, public and voluntary sector organizations dedicated to public service and helping less fortunate people and animals. But do ethics have any place in businesses that must make a profit to survive? If so, are they an 'optional extra', which you can afford only when the business prospers, or should they be at the root of a business, akin to the election manifesto of a political party?

Over the centuries, businesses have taken many different positions on these questions. Some have shifted their ground as the organizational context in which they operate has changed, even within the working lives of their founders.

For the directors of modern limited companies, which control the vast majority of economic activity, are there any duties and obligations other than to make a profit while obeying the law?

Activity 20

5 mins

In the list below, underline those individuals or groups to whom you believe an organization could have duties or obligations, apart from any that the law imposes. Then indicate up to a maximum of **ten priority items**, in the order of priority you would assign to them, with (**1**) as the highest priority and (**10**) for the lowest. Rate any to whom you believe a business owes no duty or obligation to as (**0**).

Young people	( )	General public	( )	Wildlife	( )
Shareholders	( )	Employees	( )	Creditors	( )
Company pensioners	( )	Charity	( )	Neighbours	( )
Disadvantaged groups	( )	Customers	( )	Environment	( )
Local community	( )	Suppliers	( )		

This Activity should have presented you with some difficult choices – the sort of difficult choices which business managers face all the time when trying to decide their priorities

In the Answers to Activities, on pages 124–25, you will find some suggestions to compare with your decisions, though it is likely you will disagree in some areas.

2 The stakeholders in an organization

What you have just done is identify some actual or potential stakeholders in an organization, ranging from the most obvious and immediate (customers shareholders, employees) to the more questionable and remote (charity, wildlife)

Stakeholders are those individuals or groups who have a valid interest in the way in which an organization conducts its affairs – including, but not exclusively, its financial health.

It is common practice in many modern organizations to identify the principal stakeholders in their organizations. Usually, this is done in broad terms and the definition will vary from one organization to another.

Activity 21

15 mins

S/NVQ C4.2

This Activity may provide the basis of appropriate evidence for your S/NVQ portfolio. If you are intending to take this course of action, it might be better to write your answers on separate sheets of paper.

Identify the stakeholders acknowledged by your own organization. You may find them in documents including:

■ annual reports and employee editions of annual reports;
■ mission statements and/or policy statements posted on general notice boards;
■ employee handbooks;
■ job descriptions;
■ induction training procedures.

Note down whether you believe the correct stakeholders have been identified, or whether:

- some have been included that you would have omitted;
- *or* there are others you would have included that are missing.

If no such statement exists for your own organization (and this is not a legal requirement in the way that exhibiting some safety information is):

- draw up a list of a maximum of five or six groups whom you believe have a claim to be considered as stakeholders;
- discuss them with your immediate manager to see if you are in broad agreement – bearing in mind that you work for the same organization.

2.1 Actions or deeds

Whether or not your organization identifies their stakeholders on paper is less important than what it does in practice. Not every company has the inclination, or the resources, to write everything down, but that does not mean that it is not inclined to take its wider obligations and duties seriously.

Assuming that your organization does identify stakeholders, whether formally or not, the likelihood is that they will include:

- shareholders;
- customers/suppliers;
- employees/company pensioners;
- neighbours/neighbouring sites/local community;
- the environment/wider community.

These are frequently the identified groups to whom organizations accept they have obligations and duties to.

- Shareholders have invested often large sums of money (relative to their own resources) and have a right to know that it is being used wisely and for purposes they approve, as well as within the legal requirements described in Session A. The law cannot 'tell' every limited company how to run its affairs. A judge may think it unwise for a company to spend 90% of its revenues on TV advertising, or in buying up speculative stocks of raw materials, but he or she will not say they cannot do this, unless it is outside their memorandum of association to do so (highly unlikely) or the directors have broken the terms of the articles of association (very unlikely).
- Customers have a right to expect many things of their suppliers, including prompt, courteous service, consistent quality standards and continuity of

supply not prejudiced by unwise speculations or poor management of people or resources. There is an obligation to treat suppliers fairly, to pay invoices on time and not to use them as sources of free credit.

■ Employees may have invested years of their lives in the organization, as may their families. They may also have bought shares, or invested in company pension schemes. Company directors have obligations to them when offering share option schemes, or encouraging them to join pension schemes.

■ Neighbours' lives and businesses can be affected adversely by noise or other disturbances, which may not be sufficient to exceed any legal thresholds, but still affect the lives of many people and their businesses. Where an employer is the major employer for a whole community, as many coal mines, steel works, engineering companies and insurance companies have been (and as Enron was in America), they may be considered to have an obligation to the people who have contributed to their business often over many years.

■ There may be obligations to the wider community and the environment generally, even though there is no specific legal requirement.

> Many employees of companies, including Enron, have lost both their jobs and their savings when their employer's businesses collapsed. The directors of such companies should surely have considered such potential catastrophic effects when taking decisions that might affect employees.

3 Ethics in practice

Looking at the stakeholders that an organization identifies gives you a good basic idea of its ethical stance. If it identifies none, or if its actions indicate that it recognizes none, this in itself indicates its stance on issues outside legal requirements.

But why should an organization, particularly one that has to make a profit, do any more than the law requires anyway? Many do, but should those that choose not to be condemned. Or is it nobody's concern but their own and that of their shareholders?

3.1 Value judgements

This leads directly into the difficulty of making judgements based on subjective, as opposed to objective, criteria.

Activity 22

Two large employers, both plcs, employed more than 80% of the adult population of a large town. Both offered 'share option' schemes to all permanent employees. Which do you think was the better employer – Company A or Company B?

- **Company A** supported many community initiatives, had a subsidized staff restaurant, provided health care facilities to all employees, contributed to the staff pension scheme and helped organize a thriving sports and social club for staff and former employees. It made a 6 per cent return on total assets; paid regular but modest dividends to shareholders and was rated ' dull' by city analysts on its share price performance. Its safety statistics were slightly worse than the industrial sector average.

- **Company B** took no part in local activities, closed its staff restaurants some years ago, offered no health facilities to staff and did nothing to encourage the social club run by employees on their own initiative. It did offer a pension scheme and contributed on a modest scale to 'top up' employees' contributions. It made 9% on total assets, paid above average dividends to shareholders and was recommended for investment by prudent city analysts. Its safety record was rather better than the industrial sector average – a 'higher risk' sector than Company A.

As with so many questions involving the 'style' that companies adopt, there is no right answer that can be justified purely on objective grounds.

- From the viewpoint of a shareholder, or a Health and Safety inspector, Company B might well be the choice because of its better financial performance and safety record. But some shareholders might disapprove of its perceived lack of concern for employees in their community.
- From one employee's point of view, the good facilities and activities available outside work provided by Company A might make it a better place to work. But another might feel that they should put more thought into preventing accidents and assuring the future by making better returns for the shareholders – and the many company pensioners who depended on them.

Your decision as to which is the 'better' employer will depend on your personal experience, preferences and ethical values. It comes down to a matter of **value judgement.** This might cause one individual to refuse to work for a tobacco company, or an arms manufacturer, however good the employer may be. In comparison, another might say that what the company does is of no concern, provided that it operates within the 'law of the land'.

Activity 23 · 3 mins

Look at the statements below and decide which of them are subjective **value judgements**. You need no knowledge of the topics to make a correct choice. Underline the value judgements you select.

1   This is the worst team England have ever put on the field.

2   Sir Donald Bradman achieved the highest average runs per innings ever recorded in a test match career.

3   Lester Piggot rode more Derby winners than any other jockey in history.

4   Pavarotti is the best tenor there has ever been.

5   Victory in the Falkland Isles was the finest feat of arms in military history.

6   Elvis Presley was the greatest singer of all time.

7   Red Rum won three Grand Nationals, more than any other horse in history.

You can check your answers on page 125. The distinguishing feature is that you cannot measure the 'value judgements' in any arithmetical way.

■   How do you compare a modern singer such as Pavarotti with generations for whom there are no recordings available, or one military campaign with all the others which have taken place over thousands of years?

■   Objective statements simply give the facts; it is a matter of record that the three sports personalities named did what was claimed. If the statement read 'Lester Piggot rode the winners of ten Derbies', that could be checked and proved inaccurate – as a matter of fact, he rode nine. Saying he was the 'finest jockey there has ever been' is a matter of opinion.

There is nothing wrong in making value judgements – everyone has to do so throughout their lives. Problems arise when people confuse their factual judgements with their opinions. These are a reflection of their upbringing, experience, intrinsic preferences, and perceptions of right and wrong.

The statements in Activity 23 were deliberately kept to what should be non-contentious topics. But, as you will know from your own experience, value judgements over the perceived merits of sporting teams, pop stars, flower arrangements and vegetable marrows can quickly lead to heated discussions. The extent to which the argument is important is forgotten once it becomes a contest between people holding different opinions.

There is no objective answer as to what is 'best' or 'worst', and about what is 'right' or 'wrong', that is acceptable to everyone. Consequently, there is no way of settling the point that neither party can rationally deny is true. The argument can continue, until both parties weary of it, or at worst come to blows.

3.2 Personal ethics and business ethics

The examples of tobacco and armaments raise the question of potential conflicts between people's personal moral codes and those of potential employers. Most people take a 'common sense' view of such issues, not expecting to agree with everything their employer does. But, sometimes the gap between the values of employers and employees can be too great.

A large company manufactured a wide range of food products for national companies. Their range included pies, pasties, sausage rolls and other items containing meat. None of their products was sold under the company's own name and it was not obvious from outside what their factory did.

Over a period of time, staff, who were vegetarians on religious grounds, were recruited . No mention of what the company did was made to them and all left as soon as they found out what their jobs would involve. This was expensive for the company and upsetting for the people recruited.

'Synergy' is a word often used to indicate the degree of fit that exists between, for example:

- two companies that are thinking of merging;
- an employee and his or her employer.

This true story shows simply that there needs to be some **synergy** between the ethical values of a business and the people whom it employs. As a rule of thumb, employees need to be generally in accord with the ethics of their employers for more than half the time.

If employees face a 'dilemma a day' over the employer's actions which, though perfectly legal, conflict with their own moral beliefs, then perhaps they should think of moving to an employer with whom they feel more comfortable, or have greater synergy.

Of course, it may not be that simple for an individual. The issues are not always as clear cut as a religious objection to handling meat, or an aversion to working with alcohol because of its potential to harm people.

What do you do if there is no other job available and there are financial pressures on you?

Or, should you work from the inside to mitigate the effects of activities, which though objectionable to you, will continue to happen however wrong you believe them to be ?

Members of one animal charity did just that. It was opposed to the slaughter of animals for human consumption but the members were asked to monitor the way in which abattoirs were run to ensure that animals were treated and despatched as humanely as possible under the circumstances.

It is hard to understand how people could undertake work in circumstances so repugnant to them. They presumably did so to mitigate the effects of actions that they knew they could not prevent, unless the attitudes of the majority of people throughout society changed. In this case, individuals subordinated their own feelings for what they perceived to be a greater good.

In many areas of business activity, employees and employers frequently have to make 'least worst' decisions.

4 Mission statements

EXTENSION 2
This provides a sample mission statement, based on those which appear regularly on company notice boards.

Mission statements have been referred to already. You may be familiar with your own organization's and those of other organizations with which it deals. Sometimes, similar documents are referred to as 'credos'.

4.1 Forms of mission statement

Both **mission** and **credo** – which comes from the Latin meaning 'I believe' – have religious connotations, which may or may not be helpful.

In fact, mission statements have been used in one form or another, outside organized religion, for a long time. The BBC, the UK's largest and most influential broadcasting organization, has a mission under its governing charter:

'To educate, to inform, to entertain'.

This was proclaimed by Lord Reith, the BBC's first and most influential Director General, in the 1930s and says concisely what it still aims to do over 70 years later.

In framing their visions of what their organizations were about, Lord Reith managed to say a great deal in a very few words. By contrast, look at the mission statement provided as Extension 2, which is not untypical of the modern statements you may see.

Activity 24

10 mins

S/NVQ C4.1, C4.2

This Activity may provide the basis of appropriate evidence for your S/NVQ portfolio. If you are intending to take this course of action, it might be better to write your answers on separate sheets of paper.

- If your organization has a mission statement, or credo, obtain a copy, and write a short assessment of its effects on the organization's day-to-day activities, as you see them.

- If your organization does not have a mission statement, refer to the one provided as Extension 2. Suggest briefly how, if at all, it might be adapted to match your perceptions of the ethics of your organization. You may find it helpful to refer back to the stakeholders identified in Activity 21, as the key to whom the document should address.

The John Lewis Partnership – now a plc – has traded in its many department stores under the banner 'Never knowingly undersold' for many years. If you can find goods of the same description and quality in someone else's store, they will refund the difference – it's guaranteed. (However, buying 'on line' is not covered.)

In general terms, the shorter the statement, the greater its impact and the more powerful it will be as a focal point for all activities. The organization's ethical stance can be summed up in phrases such as:

- 'least cost producer – always';
- 'customers, first, last and always'
- 'never knowingly undersold'
- 'people before profits'
- 'saving the environment'
- 'low prices permanently' – which Asda has engraved in 'tablets of stone' in their store entrances – another biblical reference.

Ideally, they should represent a rallying point, like the regimental colours. No matter how thorny the problem, a manager should be able to point to the credo' and say simply, 'That's our banner. That's where we start from – we must address the issue in those terms. I don't need to ask higher management – they've told me what they believe right there.'

Statements that express succinct, credible organizational goals, and are achievable with effort are a valid way for an organization to set out its stall for dealings with its identified stakeholders.

When mission statements run to more than 200 words, as the example in Extension 2 does, they begin to lose their bite.

4.2 The pitfalls

If a mission statement becomes a string of pious platitudes, which the organization patently doesn't believe in, and cannot or will not commit the resources to achieving, then it will probably do more harm than good. The language of mission statements is rooted in religious concepts, so it is as well for those who devise them to remember that 'the road to hell is paved with good intentions'.

5 Is good ethics good business?

There is no need to rely on value judgements when trying to answer this question. There is plenty of objective evidence about organizations that go far beyond what the law requires to enable you to compare them with those that do not.

5.1 The law and ethics

The United Kingdom has laws that have developed over many centuries. It gave universal voting rights to all adult citizens early in the twentieth century. Consequently, statute law tends to reflect what is morally acceptable to the majority of citizens most of the time. Therefore, an organization that says it will do no more than what the law requires is still in practice tied to an ethical framework in every aspect of its activities touched by statute law. Even so, many organizations go far beyond what the law requires – an ethical tradition that has existed for centuries.

5.2 Organizations that do more than they have to

Long before the law intervened in matters of health, safety and welfare, Robert Owen, a Welshman who owned the New Lanark Cotton Mills on the Clyde in Scotland, established a humane system of management and welfare provisions for employees that was far removed from the ethics of the 'master and servant' laws which then were in force. Decent conditions of work and housing were provided for employees and Owen was a model employer.

The mills at New Lanark still exist and can be visited, close by the beautiful Falls of Clyde. They are a lasting monument to Owen's foresight and philanthropic instincts.

Farther south, near Bradford, Titus Salt, a self-made woollen manufacturer, created an entire model town, Saltaire, complete with library, public park, and lecture and concert halls. Again, working and welfare provisions were far better than required by the rudimentary safety and public health legislation of the time.

Saltaire is considered a highly desirable place to live in; the town became a world heritage site in 2001, 150 years after its founder created it.

For every philanthropist, there were many more employers who waited until the law intervened to make them improve their standards. But some very large businesses of the twenty-first century have their roots in those which believed that their 'stakeholders' included employees as well as customers and shareholders.

Activity 25 · 5 mins

Can you name four or five commercial companies currently flourishing whose founding fathers took a strong ethical stance on issues such as:

- their responsibilities to the wider community;
- the welfare of employees and the purity of their products?

Look for companies founded in the nineteenth, or early twentieth, centuries. Include any local examples in your area, as well as national or international organizations.

_____

_____

_____

_____

There are many examples of ethically based businesses which have achieved long-term success, so your answer will probably have included different names from those below. However, many of the ones listed are still household names a century or more after they were founded by people who perceived profit as a long-term affair.

- **Cadbury Schweppes**
  The original Cadbury business was run by a Quaker family, who provided both a model factory and a model town (Bournville, near Birmingham) which is still a desirable place to live.

- **Unilever**
  The Lever family also created a model town – Port Sunlight (named after a brand of soap) with a fine art gallery and many facilities for employees. The town still exists and the company is now one of the largest in its sector world-wide.

■ **John Lewis Partnership**

The company has a very singular management structure, in which all permanent employees have a stake. It provides many facilities for current and ex-employees and is still one of the UK's most successful retailers.

■ **Tate & Lyle**

The sugar refiners have a continuing involvement with the local community in East London and provide employment to many people in poorer countries from which they buy raw material as Europe's only cane sugar refiner. Henry Tate founded art galleries in London and Liverpool, with whom they also have close connections. Abram Lyle was another generous philanthropist.

■ **Price's candles**

The Price family created much of Battersea, in south-west London, as a decent place to live for employees at their candle factory by the River Thames. Their brand is still a leader in candle making, although the firm has since changed hands.

■ **Rank Hovis McDougall**

The Rank family, who came from the Hull area of Yorkshire, still have close links to the local community through the flour-milling company that bears their name. They are amongst the largest flour millers in Western Europe.

One acid test of success for a business is long-term viability. Your answers, and the list provided above, show that ethical approaches to business can produce a long-lasting financial payback, even if they increase costs in the short term. Your list may include different names and hopefully examples of local businesses which have believed that they had responsibilities to stakeholders other than owners and shareholders.

There are many examples in the USA of capitalists, industrialists and entrepreneurs who have taken the broader view of what a commercial organization's responsibilities should be.

> **The Hershey Corporation**
>
> Hershey is the largest manufacturer of chocolate confectionery in the USA. It was founded by William Hershey, in Pennsylvania, in 1894. He used the profits to found a school for orphans, which now educates more than 1,200 children per year and has endowments of around £3.5 billion, making it richer than most American universities. The whole town of Hershey, named after the founder, depends on the corporation's activities.
>
> In 2002 the company was the subject of a possible take-over bid involving Nestlé, the Swiss multi national company — the world's largest food company — and Cadbury Schweppes, themselves

Enlightened employers tend to regard developing their employees as an investment in the future. The payback may take many years, but so does investment in expensive equipment. The current Investors in People programme, to which ILM subscribes, starts from a similar ethical standpoint.

Other American benefactors to the wider community include Bill Gates and Andrew Carnegie. Bill Gates, founder of Microsoft, has spent enormous sums on educational and research facilities. Andrew Carnegie (1835–1919) , a Scot by birth, made a vast fortune from iron manufacturing in the USA, with a reputation as a ruthless businessman. His philanthropy has funded educational institutions, libraries and museums in the USA and across the world.

successors to another business with philanthropic origins. Ironically, the Hershey Trust, which owned 30% of the stock, was more keen to sell than other stockholders. The Trust feared over-dependence on a single company in the falling stockmarket of 2002. That claim was disputed by many Hershey employees, stockholders and former pupils at the school.

Eventually, the take-over bid was blocked successfully in the courts. The Hershey case study illustrates how convoluted questions of business ethics can become.

Most businesses which are going to fail do so within a few years of starting up. So, it is evident that businesses built on strong ethical foundations can be very long-lived. However, there are many other long-established businesses that would not claim to have any particular ethical roots.

Because standards of morality change, companies that are in themselves model employers can become regarded as pariahs almost no matter what they do.

Tobacco manufacturers are often now seen in that way. Yet:

■ their business activities are perfectly legal in the United Kingdom;
■ governments of all parties are happy to draw enormous revenues from them;
■ much of their raw material is grown in poorer parts of the world, where they provide employment to people who need it.

By contrast, **car manufacturers** in general attract a far less vitriolic press. Yet:

■ cars are the third major source of premature death throughout the world, following famine and war;
■ cars are responsible for a vast amount of pollution;
■ car-making is concentrated in fewer and fewer plants, mainly in wealthy countries.

Business ethics involves making value judgements all the time. There are very few 'right' answers, if right means accepted by 100% of rational people.

Those companies that do not become involved in activities not directly related to their business could argue that their primary function is to:

■ maximize shareholder value in terms of share price growth and dividends;
■ work within the laws of the lands in which they operate;

Franklin Roosevelt, US President 1933–45, said in his inaugural address during 1933, in the depths of the worst depression America has yet known: 'We have always known that heedless self-interest is bad morals. Now we know that it is bad business.'

- pay due taxes as levied in those countries;
- provide terms and conditions of employment appropriate to those countries' laws and customs.

They might further argue that:

- it is for governments to decide on priorities for using the taxes which they raise;
- a prosperous economy will require less charitable activity and there will be more people able to contribute to it.

The Kingfisher Group, which owns B&Q in the UK, has developed a broad corporate social responsibility policy, which includes looking at safety and welfare standards for employees of suppliers throughout the world.

> **Credit Suisse First Boston (CSFB)**
>
> In 2002 CSFB, a major international bank, wrote to its employees world-wide announcing 1,750 job cuts on top of 4,800 about a year before. John Mack, the Chief Executive, wrote: 'Unfortunately in this environment, to be competitive we have no alternative. And we owe it to our shareholders.'
>
> Mr Mack is known as 'Mack the knife' and it is fairly clear from his letter what his list of stakeholders in CSFB would comprise. But if he was right and the company would otherwise fail, would retaining those 1,750 people have been a better decision as far as the remaining 20,000 plus employees worldwide were concerned? And what about the tens of thousands of people who had invested in the bank, either directly or through institutions such as pension funds?

The examples of Hershey and CSFB both demonstrate how difficult ethical decisions in business can be. Time and again, senior managers are faced with looking for 'least worst' options under difficult circumstances. The honourable ones will look for the 'greater good of the greatest number'.

5.3 Looking at motives

It is easy to become sceptical about the motivation of **all** senior executives when faced by the scandals and ensuing lawsuits that have shaken the USA's economy at the turn of the twenty-first century. The revelations of Congressional and legal investigations raise serious questions about the ethics – and legality – of much of the conduct of business leaders and has tainted many honourable people in the process. Mud, as the saying goes, sticks.

However, some of the chief executives who have tried to rescue companies such as CSFB and Marconi were not themselves involved in the decisions that caused the downfall of enormous companies. They are trying to 'pick up the pieces' left by previous managements.

C P Snow (1905–1980) was a scientist and adviser to governments in the 1960s. He wrote a series of novels about politics in universities and government, the best known of which is *Corridors of Power*, describing a moral crisis in government.

C P Snow, the writer and historian, described what he called 'the cynicism of the unworldly'. He argued it was easy for those who have never held power themselves, or had to take responsibility for big, difficult decisions, to criticize the motives of all politicians and business leaders who do.

The fact that decisions are difficult does not, unfortunately, mean that inaction is always the best course – that would be too easy in the real world.

6 Communications

Looking at an organization's actions will usually give you a better idea of what their ethical values are than reading or listening to what they say about them. Nevertheless, in the media conscious twenty-first century, it can be important for organizations to say what they are doing and why. Mission statements are a way of communicating organizational values to the identified stakeholders, but it is often necessary to do so more actively. Ways in which this can be done include:

- public relations briefings;
- annual reports.

6.1 Public relations briefings

Public relations is a management function that has grown in influence dramatically. Most large organizations have a senior manager called a 'director of communications' or equivalent title.

Through briefings of the local or national media, the organization can put across its point of view in advance, rather than reacting to events as they occur. If you are involved in team briefing in any way, you are really engaged in a similar exercise, trying to nip rumours in the bud, before they spread through the grapevine of internal communications.

Unfortunately, the attempts at total 'news management' by politicians and senior business managers around the world have made practitioners of public relations suspect. The more influential and less than scrupulous 'spin doctors' have devalued the efforts of those who are simply putting across an organization's point of view in a straightforward way. If an organization is undertaking charitable work, or investing heavily in its stakeholders, particularly those other than shareholders, there is no ethical reason to hide its light under a bushel.

- Some organizations prefer to 'do good by stealth', just as some donors to charity demand anonymity, but there is no legal or moral reason to do so.
- In fact, modern law requires organizations of all kinds to be open and 'transparent' about all their dealings, including donations to charities and political parties.

6.2 Annual reports

Organizations in the public, private and voluntary sectors are all required to issue annual reports, mostly available to anyone who cares to read them. Until recently, such reports were almost exclusively filled with the accounting and legal management data required by law. Increasingly, they are seen also as public relations documents, intended to help 'sell' the organization and its values to existing and potential stakeholders.

In fact, the reports of some organizations are being criticized for becoming too 'glossy' and hiding the important factual information behind glossy publicity photographs and 'photo opportunities' for senior executives.

Activity 26 · 15 mins

S/NVQ C4.1

This Activity may provide the basis of appropriate evidence for your S/NVQ portfolio. If you are intending to take this course of action, it might be better to write your answers on separate sheets of paper.

Obtain a copy of your own organization's annual report and/or employee report/internal newsletters or briefing sheets and identify from them:

- donations for charitable purposes;
- donations to political parties;
- support for local community programmes in education/young people, the arts, sports/physical education, health, senior citizens, the environment;
- other activities concerning wider social purposes, including overseas initiatives.

If no such documents exist for your own organization, you can obtain a copy of an annual report from any plc head office, by ringing them and asking for a copy to be sent to you. Look up the contact details of a selection of organizations on the Internet.

_____

_____

_____

_____

_____

_____

You should now have a very clear grasp of the 'ethical stance' of the organization whose literature you have examined. You may be directly involved in community initiatives sponsored by your organization. If so, that is a clear demonstration of actions speaking louder than words.

7 Political, investment and trading practices

7.1 Political donations

Many organizations have made donations to political parties over the years. Recently, these have come under scrutiny, lest there should be any expectation of favours from the receiving party. Matters such as planning permissions; tobacco advertising; and scientific trials for genetically modified (GM) crops have all been raised as concerns. Trade union donations, chiefly to the Labour Party, have also been pictured as a way of exerting undue influence.

However, as long as political parties exist, they will have to be funded somehow. While membership declines, and the possibility of funding from general taxation is still only a matter for discussion, donations are probably essential to ensuring the survival of the political system that has served the UK for more than a century. The main requirement for any UK organization to operate successfully – whether it be a business, trades union, charity or public utility – is a stable democratic political system. Organizations of any kind which make open and legally permissible donations can therefore argue that it is in their general interest to do so on behalf of all their identified stakeholders.

7.2 Investment and trading decisions

Many individuals and organizations try to take investment decisions on ethical grounds. Many will not invest in companies that are involved with tobacco, alcohol or armaments.

Public opinion, if expressed strongly enough, can bring about changes in company policy.

Activity 27 · 5 mins

Can you suggest a number of specific ways in which public opinion has resulted in changes in the following.

■ Your own organization's activities – for example, in the way that it sources raw materials or disposes of waste?

_____

_____

■ The merchandise on supermarket shelves?

_____

_____

The many examples of how public opinion has affected the merchandise on supermarket shelves include:

■ increasing numbers of free-range eggs and poultry products;
■ increasing amounts of organically produced items;
■ many cosmetics advertised as not being tested on animals;
■ items labelled as being made from renewable resources, such as 'sustainable forests';
■ more extensive labelling of products generally.

Over time, public opinion can sway the policies of democratic governments who have to keep an eye on the next ballot, unless party leaders feel strongly enough that their policies are right and the electorate is wrong. Once a government changes its mind, then corporations and companies, however powerful they may be, will have to follow suit.

Governments have intervened in the UK and elsewhere to rein in unfair trading practices, particularly those involving monopolies and the use of 'insider dealing' to make large capital gains through obtaining privileged confidential information.

One particular practice they have taken seriously is called 'predatory pricing'.

A large retailing company was losing sales to a group of local independent shops which co-operated to buy products cheaply and then sell them on at economic prices, undercutting the larger company's stores in the area. The small shops involved sold only a restricted range, but in a market that was highly profitable to the larger stores, whose market share in the area declined significantly.

The large company decided to eliminate the competition. It ran a high-profile campaign in its stores, offering the goods involved at a price below the one it paid for them. It was big enough to take the loss for an extended period of several months. Customers moved away from the smaller outlets and several of them closed, or moved into other business activities. The large group then systematically restored its profit margins to their original levels – there was no longer any competition to fear.

This example is hypothetical, but the practice it describes has been used by many would-be monopolists to drive out competition, or bring it to heel. Even the people who adopt such practices would probably not describe them as 'good ethics'. They just think of them as good business – for them, at any rate.

This kind of predatory trading is illegal, but there are organizations that will try to find ways around the legislation in ways less obvious than in the example.

If you happen to work for one of these organizations and dislike what you see happening, what can you **do** about it?

8 The Public Interest Disclosure Act (PIDA) 1999

If you feel strongly enough about something your organization is doing, have sufficient moral courage – and preferably hard information to support your case – then you might take action under PIDA .

This Act is commonly known as the 'Whistleblowing Act' and protects employees who act in good faith.

> In 2002, a confidential survey revealed that many senior managers in the Health Service were unhappy with the way in which senior managers were managing to ensure that they met government targets. If their concerns are genuine and they act in good faith, they might be able to make a 'protected disclosure' under the PIDA legislation.

- In July 2000 Toni Fernandes was awarded £293,000 by an employment tribunal as compensation for unfair dismissal. He was a senior accountant with a large organization and had been dismissed for 'blowing the whistle' on his employer about a range of dubious financial practices over an extended period. After he disclosed his fears under the provisions of PIDA, he was dismissed and took his case to the tribunal.
- Leslie Holden, a train driver, was awarded £48,000 in 2001 by a tribunal for constructive dismissal. He had reported that drivers worked long hours and sometimes fell asleep in their cabs. His employer ignored his claims and took retaliatory action against him which the Tribunal decided amounted to constructive dismissal.
- Kathryn Bolkovac was paid substantial undisclosed damages in 2002 by her employer – the United Nations (UN) – after an employment tribunal decided she was unfairly dismissed for reporting links between UN staff and the sex trade in Bosnia. It involved young girls from the community which the UN was in Bosnia to protect. The tribunal ruled there was no doubt that Ms. Bolkovac had made a 'protected disclosure' under the Act and had been dismissed unfairly for reporting her concerns.

8.1 What the Act aims to achieve

The Act was introduced to help people who are wrestling with their consciences because of information they have about aspects of their organization's activities. It provides protection against dismissal or other disciplinary action. It is enforced via the Employment Tribunal system, as are complaints concerning alleged unfair dismissal for any other reason. The Act is not intended to be a channel for every minor grievance that an employee may have, and they should use any internal channels available to them first.

There must be a genuine public interest to make 'blowing the whistle' a 'qualifying disclosure' under the Act.

If you are ever inclined to use PIDA, it will help your case if you have exhausted any internal grievance procedures or 'hot lines' available to you before you 'pick up the whistle'.

Qualifying disclosures

The Act allows complaints to be registered about a wide range of topics. A 'qualifying disclosure' is defined as one which displays genuine concerns about crimes, civil offences (including negligence and breach of contract) miscarriage of justice, dangers to health, safety and the environment – and the attempted cover-up of any or all of these.

Activity 28

S/NVQ C4.1, C4.3

This Activity may provide the basis of appropriate evidence for your S/NVQ portfolio. If you are intending to take this course of action, it might be better to write your answers on separate sheets of paper.

■ Think about your own organization and the channels open to you for raising sensitive issues relating to: bad practices that are a common aspect of working life and condoned by local management; policies and procedures that do not exist but which you believe should.
The examples given where people have resorted to 'whistleblowing' legislation may help you decide which areas could benefit from attention in your own workplace.

■ List the channels presently open to you to raise such issues, other than by direct communication with your immediate boss.

_____

_____

_____

■ Note down what additional channels you believe could improve the communications process for sensitive issues that staff may be nervous about raising.

_____

_____

_____

9 Conflicts and ethical dilemmas

It is often easier to express moral outrage from the sidelines than to raise ethical issues with your employers. Organizations themselves may also be guilty of not confronting ethical issues.

■ A large international corporation, famed for its children's films, found itself operating a profitable soft porn TV channel when it acquired another company. It was not broadcasting illegal material.

Should the corporation have closed down the channel – or sold it, in which case someone else would continue to operate it – or carry on and take the profits?

The profit motive and business ethics may sometimes seem to be in conflict.

■ An animal charity, dedicated to vegetarian practices, sold bone china mugs as a part of its fund raising merchandise. A supporter pointed out that bone china contained animal bones.

The charity now sells only earthenware mugs. But many of its supporters probably wear leather shoes, or drive cars with leather seats, or use leather leashes when they take their dogs for walks.

As an individual you will also be faced with similar ethical dilemmas.

Activity 29

7 mins

Look at each of the following scenarios and underline the course of action you honestly think you would follow.

Personal dilemmas

■ Your religion and upbringing forbid you to eat or come into contact with prescribed animal products and seafood. The company decides to diversify from a range that doesn't include such items into one that does.

Would you: **do nothing; complain to the company; resign**?

■ You work in the bought ledger department of a large company. It regularly pays its suppliers up to three months late and requires you to feed them a range of excuses which you know are untrue. The company always pays your salary on time.

Would you: **do nothing; complain to the company; resign**?

■ You know that the garage in which you work flouts many of the safety guidelines it should follow in using hazardous equipment. When you complain, you are told it is 'none of your business' and it 'saves precious time'.

Would you: **do nothing; use the 'PIDA' act; resign**?

■ Some members of your team frequently 'clock each other in' and falsify job sheets to claim payment for work not done. They are of the same ethnic origin as yourself, which is different from that of the company's owners and senior management.

Would you: **do nothing; have a 'quiet word'; take formal action**?

Organizational dilemmas

Imagine yourself to be the Chief Executive of a large company facing the following situations.

■ You have a call centre network in the UK. Your largest competitor has moved business to India to save 80% of the salary bill. Many of your staff are of Indian descent.

Would you: **decide to live with your present salary bill; follow suit; consult the workforce**?

■ Your company is struggling and needs to save money. For years it has supported the local community at a cost averaging £200,000 a year – 0.5 per cent of your total spending.

Would you: **continue to contribute; ask shareholders' opinions; reduce or cut spending**?

■ By spending £75,000 on dust extraction equipment, you could reduce emissions to the atmosphere significantly. You are not in breach of the law and your business makes money.

Would you: **wait till standards change; do it now anyway; do it and save money on staff costs**?

It is much easier to pose ethical questions than to find answers which will satisfy everyone. In this Activity you were deliberately confronted with **personal** dilemmas as well as **organizational** ones, and in all cases you were asked to answer as though **you** had personal responsibility for taking the decision of whoever was in the 'hot seat'.

9.1 Corporate responsibility – no place to hide?

Even the largest plc, though a distinct legal entity, can act only through the people who run it at every level, which is why Lord Denning, the distinguished judge, framed the concept of the 'directing mind'. This is effectively the 'top' manager who must – or should – take ultimate responsibility for its actions, just as a sole proprietor must for a much smaller business.

The law is increasingly unwilling to allow senior managers to hide under layers of management – and the delayering process which many have set in train actually leaves them with fewer places to hide, as well as fewer managers.

Under UK law, ignorance of the law is no defence. Neither, increasingly, is ignorance of practices which, though not illegal, may be unethical and unfairly disadvantage or deceive competitors or any of the stakeholders in a business.

9.2 Personal responsibility

Though senior managers must take ultimate responsibility for many aspects of an organization's actions, they are not the instigators of every wrongful action that it takes. Managers at all levels and all employees contribute to the prevailing organizational culture (which we will be examining in Session C) and should take responsibility for actions which:

- support illegal unethical policies;
- or flout legal and ethical ones

President Harry Truman of the USA 1945 –1953, had a sign in his office that read:

> 'The buck stops here.'

It was an admirable sentiment and is as good a thought as any to leave you with at the end of this session on business ethics and personal responsibility.

Self-assessment 2

20 mins

1   Complete the following sentence.

Four potential groups of stakeholders in an organization are _____

_____, _____, _____ and_____.

2   Complete the sentence, using the words **facts**, **value**, **opinions**, **objective**.

_____ judgements are based on _____ whereas _____ judgements are based on _____.

3   When an individual's values correspond broadly with those of the organization for which he or she works, it may be said that **conflict** exists between them. Do you agree or disagree with this sentence and if so why?

_____

_____

_____

4   Complete the following sentence.

There are many examples of organizations which have combined a sense of _____ responsibility with _____ term commercial _____.

5   Put the phrase 'the cynicism of the unworldly' into your own words.

_____

_____

_____

6   Select the appropriate phrase to complete the following sentence: (a) a slick (b) an ineffective (c) a professional (d) a discredited.

Public relations briefings are _____ way of communicating the organization's values to the wider world.

7   The 'Whistleblowing Act' is a nickname for which piece of legislation? Which legal institution deals with complaints under it?

_____

_____

8   Name three possible matters which could be dealt with under the 'Whistleblowing Act'.

_____

_____

_____

Answers to these questions can be found on pages 121–22.

10 Summary

- This session has tackled some of the hardest questions which human beings face in every aspect of life. Its principal objective has been to make you to think hard about them in every aspect of **your** life.

- There are no **right** answers to the majority of ethical questions – in the way that a problem in arithmetic or trigonometry has one answer. Fundamentally decent people can disagree violently over ethical questions.

- Many organizations accept – and have always accepted – that the pursuit of self interest is not their only valid objective. They believe that groups of people other than the business's owners have a valid interest in its activities and the impact of these activities. Such organizations have frequently achieved long-term commercial success.

- Severe problems can arise when an individual's ethical values are irreconcilably different from those of the organization for whom he or she works.

- Changes in the business areas or management style of an organization can sometimes alter the degree of **synergy** achievable and create friction.

- The law in the United Kingdom reflects the ethical values which the majority of citizens are prepared to accept. As such, it provides a reasonable standard for organizations to adopt, though in practice many go far beyond what they **have** to do.

- **Mission statements**, or **credos**, can be a valid way of stating an organization's core beliefs. If too long, they become less effective in doing so. In any event the organization should be judged by what it does, not by what it says.

- The Public Interest Disclosure Act (1999) prevents an employer suppressing disclosure of unfair or unsafe practices by employees who fear victimization if they speak out. Provided the employees act in good faith, and preferably exhaust all internal procedures available to them, they have very strong legal protection.

- However large an organization may be, the law seeks to identify a **directing mind** which can be held accountable for its acts, whenever and wherever they happen.

Session C
Organizational culture and its effect on performance

1 Introduction

Two superficially similar organizations can have the same stated aims and organizational structure, yet give a very different impression to those who deal with them from the outside and to the people who work for them.

The difference is often explained by saying that Organization 'A' has a different culture from that of 'B'.

A definition of culture

The word culture comes from a Latin word, 'cultus', meaning a 'system of religious belief and worship'. The word is also linked to training, discipline, horticulture, agriculture – and the growing of micro organisms in a laboratory.

The religious element is a reminder of concepts such as mission statements and credos. In some companies, for example, in Japan, morning assemblies and the singing of company songs, and recital of the company mission, have unmistakable quasi religious overtones. But have they really won over the hearts and minds of their employees?

If they haven't, problems will arise when the organization's culture clashes with the beliefs and value systems of its managers and employees.

Organizational politics

This book deals with politics with a 'small p'. Party politics are outside its scope, though there may be an overlap where the interests of government, political parties and private organizations meet.

Politics may be defined as the science of civil government.

However, anyone who works for any organization will know that politics rears its head everywhere and will probably agree with Aristotle, who said: 'Man is by nature a political animal.'

Politics in practice is more art than science, the art of 'getting things done' without using brute force available to tyrants. It is something that **all** managers are involved with.

> Aristotle was writing between 380 and 320 BC, well over 2,000 years ago. Nothing significant seems to have changed about human nature since.

> Otto von Bismarck (1815–1898), the architect of German unification in the nineteenth century, said that 'Politics is the art of the possible.' It is as good a working definition as any.

- From senior management's perspective, it is the art of convincing perhaps thousands of people to commit themselves to their objectives and desired courses of action.
- From many employees' perspectives, it is the art of modifying corporate objectives and instructions to suit themselves, or in extreme cases of thwarting them entirely.

In this session, we will explore organizational culture and politics and the practical effects that they have on every organization, for good or ill.

2 Contrasting organizational cultures

Even members of the same family can create widely differing cultures within organizations:

> Two sons inherited a very large established business from their father, its founder. He was a deeply religious man who took a paternalistic approach to employees and a broad view of his social responsibilities to the wider community.
>
> The business was diverse when his sons took it over and they soon began to develop individual aspects of it. In a matter of years, they had created two separate businesses.

Business A, pursued by the younger son, Bill, continued along the lines of the founder. Wages were fairly low, job security certain, conditions of employment good, with an occupational health service available to all. Most promotions were made from within. The company contributed to various charitable causes and looked after its pensioners. It established a research institute and endowed universities to carry out fundamental research.

Business B, run by the elder son, Ben, developed a small company acquired more or less by accident some years ago, in a very different field. He did so by ruthless control of avoidable costs and by buying in aggressive sales personnel from rival companies. They had to perform to survive and the organization became known for its hire and fire tactics. The company did no more than was necessary within the law in terms of employment conditions. Most senior executives were head-hunted from rivals, which Ben felt was a cheaper way of keeping ahead of the competition than doing research.

> The examples of companies described here are based on real business organizations, which are still operating.

Both businesses prospered and it was said frequently that:

- Business A always employed twice as many people as it needed but paid them half what their jobs were worth;
- Business B employed half as many as it needed, but paid each of them twice the going rate for as long as they were there.

They illustrate how different the cultures of organizations can be, even when their owners are closely related.

Some years later, Business A found itself locked in competition with a rival – Business C – for a market in which buyers dominated. True to its lights, the company proceeded cautiously, refusing to offer high discounts and other deals to buy business. Its profit margins held up, but sales declined.

Business C adopted the opposite approach, urging sales personnel to do anything necessary to increase sales and market share. In the process, its profit margins plummeted.

When executives of the two companies met, as they did occasionally on industry-wide committees, it became a standing joke between them that:

- Business A had profit margin (M) without sales volume (V), *whereas*
- Business C had sales volume (V) without profit margin (M).

You may think that the end result for both companies – (V) × (M) was much the same – and arithmetically it more or less was.

But, both companies, in difficult circumstances, were pursuing logical strategies flowing from the respective beliefs and values of their senior managements. Had either tried to adopt their competitor's strategy, they would have created confusion amongst staff who had grown up in their respective cultures.

If your entire training and experience of business has been directed towards caution, growth from within and respect towards older and wiser colleagues, you will find it hard to become a 'swashbuckling entrepreneur' – and vice versa.

2.1 Is there one 'right' culture?

Is there one 'right' culture which is suitable in all circumstances?

You can decide what you think, based on the following Activity.

Activity 30 · 5 mins

Imagine you are in each of the following sets of circumstances and then select the cultural style that you believe would be the most likely to produce a successful outcome.

1   A company is in deep financial trouble, in a shrinking market and needing to make savage cuts to its workforce. The company is fully unionized and it will be necessary to negotiate each plant closure line by line. If the workforce are not convinced, a major strike could ensue, which would bankrupt the company and close its business entirely.

2   An organization wishes to develop a small, successful company that it has just acquired in the USA. It aims to turn its brand into a major regional force in New York State and the adjoining east coast states.

3   Two retail companies of similar size, formerly competitors, have merged and the joint management wishes to consolidate the resulting business and stabilize it before trying to expand. Where they are trading more or less against each other, some outlets will close, but only around 5% of the combined workforce will be affected.

The cultural styles from which you are asked to choose are as follows.

paternalistic	go-getting	gradualist	task-centred
swashbuckling	individualistic	benign	adventurous
team-centred	cautious	autocratic	Machiavellian

Niccolo Machiavelli lived from 1469–1527 in what is now Italy. He wrote *The Prince* in 1513, a series of essays on the realities of power, politics and leadership, which is still readable and relevant almost 500 years later. Unfortunately, 'Machiavellian' is used as a synonym for 'devious', as though he was advocating the practices he described. In fact, he was describing what he saw in the courts of Florence, Venice, Rome and the other city states of the time.

Situation 1: _____

Situation 2: _____

Situation 3: _____

You will find some suggestions in the Answers to Activities on page 125.

Bear in mind that you have been asked to make value judgements and it may be that your judgements differ from the suggestions. But you probably agreed that different cultures would be appropriate to the different situations.

As with the organizational structures that we reviewed in Session A, there is no 'one size that fits all'.

In situation 1, a swashbuckling, go-getting culture would almost certainly lead to disaster. It would also be inappropriate in situation 3 – a merger – where suspicions will be at their height between people who have been sworn enemies for years. However, such a culture could be appropriate to the expansionist aims of the American company in situation 2.

The merger between Beauclerks and Elmers into Bellesfines

Several years after a merger between two retail companies, Beauclerks and Elmers, a staff meeting was held to discuss Christmas trading activity for that season. Many staff still remained from the pre-merger days, especially in site manager roles where staff turnover was virtually nil.

The staff remaining from the two companies formed themselves into distinct groups and sat on different sides of the central aisle. They still regarded themselves as being 'Beauclerks people' or 'Elmers people' – and 'never the twain should meet'.

The companies had not only been rivals, but had very different cultures. Beauclerks had been dedicated to high quality; Elmers to low prices.

The Beauclerks staff tended to look down on those from Elmers, and the Elmers staff thought of their former rivals as snobs.

- In the ten years following the merger, the merged management had failed to bridge the gulf between the two camps, which preserved a hostile truce at best whenever they met.
- Though the particular meeting concerned arrangements for the season of good will, little was evident in the planning meeting.

This case study is based on real events, though the company names have been changed. A fact which must be recognized about organizational culture is that it can be deep-rooted, as are national, religious or personal cultures.

2.2 Cultural change

A particular culture can become established quite quickly within an organization, but can be very hard, if not impossible, to change. Politicians and businessmen frequently talk about the need to change the culture of one organization or another, and many management consultants have made their fortunes trying to help them. But the results are often far from successful.

The driving force for change: top down . . .

One of the common barriers to achieving cultural change is that it is driven from the top down. In the Bellesfines case, the new senior management wanted the combined staff of the new company to put aside the prejudices and animosities of 20 years. It was very much in the interests of senior management that they should all do so. After all, senior management had organized the merger, without asking for the opinions of long-serving staff. They had changed two names into one, which no one identified with. The French-sounding name recommended by external consultants meant nothing to staff from either camp.

. . . or bottom up ?

It is much rarer for the people at the bottom of the hierarchy to express a desire for radical change. How often have you read of the workforces of two rival companies demanding that their respective companies merged? It is something which very rarely happens, so culture change is almost always imposed from the top. It is frequently resented by everyone else.

As with many dilemmas that managers face, it is far easier to diagnose than to resolve. But managers throughout an organization should be aware of the problems that may arise when the cultural norms that people have come to expect are challenged.

> How many people who resent 'change without consultation' at work impose change on their families in the same high-handed fashion? They may impose it over where to live, what car to buy, what job to take? Family members are likely to resent change just as much as they do themselves.

> In Session A we looked at hierarchies and challenged the idea that employees are there to serve their leaders, rather than be supported by them.

In common with most management challenges, communications is the key to success. In the Bellesfines case, little attempt was made to communicate what was happening and still less to explain any benefits to staff which the senior managers believed would arise. They could have done much more.

Activity 31

5 mins

Here is a list of some of the things which the Bellesfines management could have done. Weigh up each of them and note down your opinion on its aptness in the circumstances, selecting from the range of:

- very helpful;
- helpful;
- neutral – achieving little of itself;
- unhelpful;
- very unhelpful.

There is no one answer. You will probably feel that a mix of several approaches is required. The suggestions are in random order. Option 1 is not necessarily the most helpful, nor option 12 the most unhelpful. You may have had your own experience of working through a company merger and, if so, you may be able to add to the list.

OPTION	YOUR OPINION
1 Begin regular meetings of all management staff at outlet level.	
2 Issue a new mission statement.	
3 Mix staff from the two companies in each outlet.	
4 Dismiss all existing shop managers and recruit new ones.	
5 Institute a monthly company newsletter.	
6 Set up working parties of managers from the old companies to tackle the problems of integration.	
7 Scrap both old product ranges and introduce one new one.	
8 Arrange for senior managers from each old company to spend time with their new staff at outlet level.	
9 Call a mass meeting of shop managers and tell them bluntly that they will have to get used to the new order of things.	
10 Commission a consultant to design and deliver courses on managing change for all levels of management.	
11 Start weekly team briefings.	
12 Establish a works council, with 80% of members elected by staff and 20% nominated by senior management.	
Personal experiences from equivalent situations:	

You will find some suggested opinions in the Answers to Activities on page 125.

These are matters of opinion rather than fact, so you may disagree with some suggestions. However, you probably agree that:

- options 4, 7 and 9 would be very unlikely to help individually – combined in some way, they could cause chaos and confusion;
- a combination of options 1, 6, 8 and 12 could prove helpful in achieving the desired end of fusing the two formerly competing sets of people.

The Bellesfines merger involved around 400 full-time and part-time staff, of whom around 50 were shop managers. It was a relatively low-key merger, causing few redundancies and relatively minor changes to operating procedures and product ranges. The management foresaw no particular problems in merging the two organizations.

Yet a high proportion of staff were very reluctant to abandon the culture which they had become familiar with.

It illustrates the problems that can arise when cultures become deeply ingrained at any level and people who are committed to them subsequently feel threatened by external forces. It is a feature of organizations from the very smallest to the very largest, and affects the public, private and voluntary sectors, whatever their objectives and structures may be.

2.3 Management Attitude Surveys (MAS)

Like morale, which it affects directly, organizational culture is more easy to feel than to measure. Human beings can sense instinctively a climate of fear, or the kind of high morale which seems to 'crackle' like a newly lighted log fire.

This poses a problem to larger companies that employ large numbers of people on many sites. Finding out what managers think about the existing organizational culture, which they may be trying to change, is important but difficult.

Many managers will be reluctant to say what they really think to senior managers.

Organizations have used MAS to 'test the temperature'. The survey is normally in the form of a confidential questionnaire, a sort of detailed opinion poll. The MAS deals with opinions and attitudes, rather than facts and figures. Respondents are asked to make value judgements about every aspect of their organization – ethics, culture, management style, what they think of the Managing Director; **nothing** is taboo.

The survey data is collated and analysed by independent assessors, who do not disclose what individual respondents say. The findings are usually presented by department or function. This should provide a picture of varying attitudes between, say, marketing, production, research, management services and finance department staff.

You may have been involved in a MAS yourself and know the results that it produced. Widely differing outcomes emerge.

A MAS produces results which may make very unwelcome reading for the senior manager who commissioned the survey.

The use of MAS shows the lengths to which large organizations will go to measure the state of their culture and sub-cultures. In smaller organizations, it should be much simpler to do so, simply by 'walking the job' regularly. This is something that is impossible to do when you are managing a national or international company employing hundreds or thousands of managers.

3 Culture and management style

So far in this session we have looked at the overall culture that organizations exhibit, by accident or design, for example:

- the 'paternalistic' as against the 'hire and fire';
- the 'price driven' as against the 'quality first';
- the 'volume driven' as against the 'profit driven'.

Within these cultures can exist a wide variety of management styles and sub-cultures, which may or may not exhibit synergy with the organization's overall business aims.

3.1 Blame cultures in everyday life

The United Kingdom is now a much more litigious society than ever before. There is a tacit belief that whatever happens to an individual must be the fault of someone else. TV and radio carry adverts promoting 'no win, no fee' services to take action against whoever may be deemed to be to blame for whatever happened to anyone.

Whatever value judgement you may make about this general blame culture, it is a fact of life in the early twenty-first century.

So, just as in mechanics, where 'for every action there is an equal and opposite reaction', in everyday life, the blame culture has begun to produce a reaction.

Activity 32

In your experience, what have been the effects in everyday life of the tendency to assign blame for every adverse event? Note down four or five examples of where this tendency has affected you, or your local community.

_____

_____

_____

_____

_____

There are, of course, all sorts of ways in which you may have answered this question. In general, schools have cancelled activities involving the remotest physical risk; local authorities have threatened to ban window boxes and cut down 'conker' trees; some activities have been removed from municipal playgrounds; headstones have been levelled in churchyards; activity holidays for children, whether organized by schools or other bodies, have been curtailed in scope or even cancelled. Pets corners have been threatened with closure – the list can be a long one.

There is no excuse for sending a party of six-year-olds up Snowdon in a snowstorm, wearing trainers, jeans, T shirts and baseball caps for protective clothing. But reaction to 'fear of blame' goes far beyond that of eliminating activities that are inappropriate or downright dangerous. In effect, it says, 'If I don't do anything, 'they'' can't get me for it' – where 'they'' could be virtually any individual or corporate body.

Such an attitude, if it becomes prevalent, can slow things down or eventually produce paralysis where everyone is afraid to do anything.

3.2 Blame cultures at work

Blame cultures tend to produce the same effect on working life. If people know that they will be in trouble for the slightest mistake, or piece of initiative, many or most will tend to do things by the book. Many will become 'jobsworths', constantly looking over their shoulders – actually or metaphorically – to see who may be checking up on them.

Such cultures can exist within all organizational structures.

In his book entitled *Hudibras*, Samuel Butler (1612 – 1680) wrote, 'He who complies against his will, is of his own opinion still.' *Hudibras* is a satire in which he attacked the zealotry of some puritans and the imposition of their moral code on others through fear and the threat of sanctions.

- In hierarchies, staff within each tier may ensure nothing is done that is outside their specific authority. The buck is passed swiftly upwards when any decision demanding initiative arises, however much that will inconvenience internal or external customers.
- In 'wheel' organizations there is a direct link from each function to the central decision maker. If that person creates a blame culture, functional managers will ensure they do nothing without specific authorisation from the centre. This will inevitably slow down decision making and overload the central decision maker with trivial matters.
- In 'flat' or 'delayered' organizations, each team leader reports directly to a relatively senior manager. This can create the same situation as the 'wheel' does, if there is an autocrat at its hub who rules by fear and demands to be involved in every decision. Paralysis and a back-covering approach can quickly develop.

Management style of ruling by fear

Nicknames for senior executives often show how their styles are perceived. Ernest Saunders, who ran the huge Guinness group during a time of mergers and high job losses, was known as 'deadly Earnest'. As was mentioned in Session B, John Mack, head of CSFB had the nickname 'Mack the knife'.

The manager who rules by fear will encourage staff to cover their own backs and to shift any possible blame which might attach to them down to subordinates, or sideways to other departments. They will keep meticulous records of everything they do, demand authorization for every action and refuse to allow any latitude to their own subordinates.

In such a culture, braver spirits may plot and scheme to overthrow a manager whose style is dictatorial and offensive.

Activity 33

3 mins

What positive and negative effects do you think the combination of an aggressive management style towards staff and a general blame culture might have on an organization's general effectiveness?

_____

_____

_____

Probably, you suggested that such a combination could have no measurable positive effects, but many negative ones. Such a culture will make for an organization-focused approach, rather than a customer-centred (or client-centred) one. Customers or clients faced with such a culture, whether they be patients in a hospital, consumers of a public utility, children in school or buyers of insurance, will find that they figure a long way down their supplier's priority list.

Providing information to higher management to prove that staff have done what the organization required of them will come well ahead of their requirements.

Any organization which finds, whether from 'walking the job' or commissioning a MAS, that such an unhealthy culture prevails would do well to remember the following maxim.

> 'No profit is generated within a business – only cost.'

An organization must take urgent, but systematic, action to change the situation. That will almost always demand a change in management style at the very top of the organization, be it large or small.

If you find that you have a less-than-affectionate nickname equivalent to those quoted amongst your own team, then you may need to look at your own style – and the sub-culture that you are creating within the organization.

3.3 Problem-solving cultures

A problem-solving culture represents the other end of the management spectrum. There is far less dependence on formal reporting and variances calculated to many places of decimals. It may be typified by statements from senior management like 'We are where we are.'

By implication, the emphasis is on looking forward and making things better in the future. Though the phrase 'problem solving' is used, there will be an inclination to regard problems as opportunities – to thinking positively – to picturing the vessel as 'half **full**', not 'half **empty**'.

Activity 34 · 3 mins

Can you suggest a number of positive and negative effects that a problem-solving culture can produce, drawing on your own experiences wherever possible?

_____

_____

_____

_____

The chances are that you identified more positive than negative effects, such as:

■ the opportunity to take reasonable risks and try new ways of doing things;
■ the ability to be honest and admit to a mistake without fear of reprisals;
■ the likelihood of a much happier and more productive working atmosphere with people working as a team, rather than a loose assembly of self-centred, suspicious individuals.

In Session B we looked at PIDA, the 'Whistleblowing Act'. On extreme occasions, it is a way for a concerned individual to 'put their head above the parapet' – without fear of having it chopped off.

On the negative side, there may be a loss of focus on vital, but uncongenial, tasks such as making cost savings. In the UK's general culture, persistently cheerful managers, 'whistling a happy tune' whatever the circumstances, may get on people's nerves and ultimately lose their respect. Decision-making can slow down and you need to be alert to the danger that, while your team is 'reasoning together' in constructive engagement, your competitors have launched a surprise attack!

There is no management culture or style that is entirely without risk. On balance the problem-centred approach has much more to commend it than the blame culture. Problem-solving encourages integrity, initiative and a focus on the external customers and clients who are the _real_ reason for the organization's existence, whether it be a hospital, an electricity supplier, a school, an insurance company or anything else.

3.4 Empowering people throughout the organization

Empowerment implies delegation of authority **to the level at which it will have the greatest positive effect** in furthering the organization's objectives.

If a fireman at the scene of a fire had to seek authority from the fire chief five miles away to turn on a fire hydrant, it would be thought preposterous. Yet many people in large organizations, however senior their job title may sound, have been required to do similarly preposterous things because of a lack of authority.

The classic management principle states the following:

'You should never delegate responsibility without authority.'

Yet that is what happens every day in organizations ruling through fear and a blame culture. People who actually deal with customers directly may know what they **ought** to do and certainly know what the customer **wants** them to do. Yet they frequently have to seek higher authority for the most trivial of actions, such as:

- ringing back a customer who has been holding on at national rates;
- replacing defective goods plainly supplied by the organization in the absence of the supporting documentation, at least up to a determined value;
- providing technical advice within the employee's proven competence level.

Delegating authority should improve staff morale, and ultimately save senior management time and money. Empowering relatively junior staff will prevent problems which they could have dealt with immediately from coming up through the system and demanding attention from senior managers.

Activity 35

2 mins

Suggest three or four conditions that need to exist for delegation and empowerment within an organization's culture to succeed.

_____

_____

_____

_____

In general terms, you probably suggested that empowered staff must be trustworthy, which means they must be:

■ trained and accredited as necessary to do what is asked of them, and competent to deal with customers or clients, internal as well as external;
■ briefed thoroughly as to their limits of authority and able to contact help immediately if the customer requires more than they are able to provide.

They must be accountable for what they do and remember that the organization has interests too and is not always wrong. However, in too many organizations, the culture is such that an employee's 'limit of authority' is reached at zero or very close to it.

Once again, you should ask yourself whether you delegate to and empower your staff so far as your context allows — or whether you tend to hold the reins firmly in your own hands, despite what the prevalent culture in your organization may expect you to do.

3.5 Corporate responsibility and corporate culture

It is no more than an extension of the delegation principle to stress that, in reality:

> 'senior managers can *only* delegate authority.'

Senior executives who create such a climate of fear that no one dares move without personal authorisation from them, make things harder for themselves. If executives refuse to delegate and empower staff, within set limits, to take decisions for themselves, how can they possibly claim that any staff member exceeded their authority? Or that they could not be expected to know what was happening throughout a vast organization?

Organizations which 'delayer' hierarchies are putting senior executives ever closer to the firing line. If they combine delayering with an autocratic management style, they make it increasingly harder to assign culpability for anything the organization does to anyone but themselves.

Strict liability

A strict interpretation of corporate responsibility is coming ever closer, in every aspect of management, from accounting procedures and misselling of financial services to corporate manslaughter. Law-makers and courts are looking for ways through management structures, however complex, to find the 'directing mind' which must answer for corporate misdemeanours, just as a sole trader must in a smaller enterprise.

Responsibility always remains with top management, no matter how many layers they interpose between themselves and day-to-day operations. Their responsibility remains even when staff do things outside the company rules, for instance by breaching health and safety law or defrauding customers.

- If directors **knew** what was happening, they ought to have prevented it.
- If they **didn't** know, they should have made it their business to find out.

4 Sub-cultures

The larger and more scattered the organization, the harder it becomes for any individual, or group, of senior managers to impose a single set of cultural values upon it.

Even in very rigidly controlled organizations, there may be functions where it is vital that people are allowed to use their initiative and imagination. Sub-cultures may develop in research, systems development, marketing and risk management – all functions in which people must be allowed to think beyond what the organization does now, or even to 'think the unthinkable' where risks to business or personal safety are concerned

4.1 Contractors and sub-contractors

The increasing use of external contractors and agency staff to undertake a wide range of routine jobs, as well as one-off projects, adds to the possibility of alien sub-cultures developing. These may run counter to the organization's declared values and objectives.

Contractors' employees are not employed by the organizations on whose site they are working. They may have entirely different backgrounds, training, experience and attitudes. Organizations that make extensive use of contractors should aim to manage their activities to ensure that they conform to the host company's cultural norms.

To achieve this, an organization first needs to take care when selecting contractors. It must check that contractors' employees have appropriate training and conform with all legal requirements concerning accreditation and insurance as a basic condition of obtaining the contract. Contractors must also be required to select sub-contractors using the same professional processes.

Before working on site, proper induction training must be provided to leave contractors' staff in no doubt as to the cultural norms which are expected of **everyone** working for the organization.

As a first line manager you have a particularly important role to play in making this happen on a continuing basis. You should refuse to accept a lower standard from contractors' employees than you demand of direct staff in such matters as standards of dress, general conduct and observance of safety and hygiene rules. These are matters that should be covered in your organization's contract with the sub-contractors.

Activity 36

8 mins

Many organizations now employ contractors or agency staff to work on their own sites for a very wide range of activities, from routine clerical, cleaning and production tasks to projects involving draughtsmen, design or computing specialists and on to major maintenance and construction works. Any or all of these may impinge on your own working area, or areas you have previously taken responsibility for.

■ Describe any differences you have noticed between the working culture of contractors or agency staff and that of your own organization's employees. Concentrate on such aspects as:

- motivation and attitude towards the organisation's cultural values – as, for example, expressed in its mission statement or other formal declaration;
- attitude to company property, waste and quality standards;
- attitude towards customers or clients, if contact exists with them;
- attitude towards health, safety and housekeeping standards;
- time keeping, sickness absence.

_____

_____

_____

_____

■ List any steps you have taken to ensure that contractors' staff meet the 'norms' demanded by the organization. Alternatively, suggest ways in which your organization could learn from the attitudes and approaches displayed by external staff.

_____

_____

_____

_____

The sort of issues which may have arisen could include:

■ lack of continuity, with different people turning up to do a job, each having to go through an individual 'learning curve';

■ the problem that if, for example, you accept contractors coming in to work in more casual clothing than your own team's, this may lead to resentment;

■ difficulty in controlling absence anmongst staff who owe no long term allegiance to the organisation;

■ potential compromising of confidential information such as recipes, specifications and costings which may be available to people who do not have the same 'stake' in your organisation as employees who have a longer term commitment to the organisation and its continuing success.

Of course many contract and agency staff are conscientious, diligent and bring specialist skills to your organisation which may not be available within it permanently, because of cost, or simply because they are not needed at all times. Some may be covering for staff on maternity leave, away on long term sick leave or on extended holidays made available under the organisation's policies.

What is important is that everyone working for your organisation should observe the standards of conduct demanded of regular staff, otherwise morale and general standards will inevitably suffer. If you are aware of a problem which you cannot deal with directly, you need to confront the issue frankly with your own manager before it becomes serious.

4.2 Responding to sub-cultures

Sub-cultures can develop in virtually any organization, whether its official culture is autocratic, paternalistic or problem-solving in character. They may work for good or ill in the overall scheme of things, and as a first line manager you need to distinguish between them.

A group of employees may develop its own sub-culture aimed at getting things done despite an over-rigid approach from senior management. In such a situation it could be appropriate to use your influence to persuade senior management to adopt different approaches.

On the other hand, a sub-culture may develop that is quite alien – where perhaps through custom and practice a group is operating without regard to the overall health of the organization. Symptoms of such a malignant sub-culture could include:

■ spinning work out into premium-rate time;
■ taking unjustified time off for supposed sickness;
■ covering up defective work to avoid disciplinary action;
■ ignoring national speed limits in order to complete delivery rounds early.

There are any number of possibilities.

In such a situation you need to root out the malignant culture, if necessary over a period of time, seeking assistance from senior management if help from them is essential.

Activity 37

A large manufacturing site had endeavoured over several years to develop a positive, problem-solving culture, supported by an ethically based mission statement, a relaxed approach by senior managers to dress standards in the offices and a single dining room to replace three former ones. The Managing Director was happy to be called by his first name and would talk informally to any member of staff whom he met as he 'walked the job' on a regular basis. He decided to make a surprise visit to the permanent night shift and ventured into a packing department in a remote corner of the site, which he had not been to before.

Here, he found a number of things that disturbed him considerably.

- Some operatives were watching an 'adult' video in a filthy staff room on a private video set.
- A hand-made poster on a wall depicted a 'skull and crossbones' with the inscription 'The next one caught with booze is for the chop'; it was signed by the permanent night shift manager.
- An aroma of cigarette smoke hung around in the toilet block.
- A pile of sub-standard product was awaiting re-packing on the in-feed to a machine.
- On asking an operative where the manager was, he received the reply, 'Who wants him then?'. On being told it was the Managing Director, the operative retorted 'Says you – dressed like that. And I'm Winston Churchill.'

All the activities mentioned were banned under company rules.

Analyse what you think the problems were in this situation (based on real events) and what the Managing Director needed to do to about them.

Among the issues you identified may have been the following.

- The Managing Director's cultural values had not taken root on the night shift.
- A sub-culture had developed amongst a group that had never met him and thought itself 'outside the system'.
- Probably there were pressures on production targets and deadlines, which the night shift simply had to cope with as best they could.
- Difficulty in recruiting night staff or replacing absentees made managers reluctant to enquire too closely into what went on after hours.

Possible remedies included the following **problem-solving approaches**.

- Taking steps to integrate the night shift into the organization, or change to a two- or three-shift system, if practicable.
- Ensuring that targets were realistic and channels open for the night shift manager to report problems and obtain help.
- Encouraging senior managers to spend time on 'nights' and 'show the flag' to people who hardly identified with the company at all, let alone with its new cultural values.
- In general, communicating directly and regularly with the night shift as a customary aspect of managing the huge and complicated site – otherwise all the efforts put in to develop a particular culture would start to unravel.

Doing nothing is not an option. It would not, however, be helpful to **instil fear** by the following.

- Reading the riot act, issuing warning letters to all and sundry, or putting up threatening notices and posters on every available surface and notice board.
- Sacking the entire shift. They would have to be replaced – and who could say that their replacements would behave any differently? Furthermore, they would need time to learn the job.

Taking such draconian measures would run counter to the whole ethical concept which the Managing Director was trying to create – and news of them would of course be all around the site in a matter of hours.

4.3 Informality vs open (or transparent) management style

The Managing Director in Activity 37 was dedicated to an informal style of management. What many senior managers – and politicians – do is regard 'informality' and 'open style' as though they meant the same thing. They don't.

The fact that the Managing Director is on first-name terms with everyone doesn't mean that he or she tells them what is going on all or most of the time in an open manner. It isn't reasonable to expect 'openness' **all** the time and naive to suggest that it's possible. There are many things an organization does which must remain confidential, and often it will make contingency plans that may never happen, unless the contingency arises.

Managers who wear dark clothes or pin stripe suits may be as open as prudence permits, while others in casual clothes wouldn't reveal the time of day without thinking deeply about it first. It comes down to personal style, whatever clothes it may be cloaked in.

Does it matter anyway? Well, as with so much that affects culture, symbols and perceptions **do** matter. People look for inconsistencies between what an organization **says** it believes in and what it actually **does**. If there is a clash between the two, it can undermine all the effort that is put into creating a particular culture.

The Managing Director in designer denim, who happily 'glad hands' everyone and then announces a factory closure via the local radio station, is sending mixed messages to the whole organization.

There should be a reasonable degree of consistency between words and actions because **actions** will always speak more eloquently than the words.

4.4 Sub-cultures and their impacts

Sometimes sub-cultures are ignored by the person responsible for setting the 'tone' for the entire organization. However, by doing so, they risk undermining the entire value system they sought to create or continue.

Many organizations that have permitted unhealthy sub-cultures to develop have subsequently found themselves before employment tribunals, as in the following examples.

Employment tribunal awards in cases where organizational cultures contravene employment law now frequently run into tens, or hundreds, of thousands of £'s and have exceeded £1 million.

■ 'Laddish' cultures, offensive to most women (and the majority of men), have led to large awards by tribunals for sex discrimination, in organizations ranging from car manufacturers to investment banks. Pornographic videos and photographs, smutty emails, suggestive remarks, entertaining customers in dubious night clubs – all have led to substantial awards.

■ Permitting 'no go' areas into which senior managers do not enquire too closely, provided the job gets done, have led to claims of race discrimination, as have childish cultures requiring people to submit to degrading forfeits.

■ Departments where people feel excluded if they are not interested in, for example, golf, or the 'right' football team can also lead in the direction of employment tribunals.

■ 'Job and finish' cultures, which throw caution to the winds every Friday afternoon, can lead to serious accidents, prosecutions, fines or even imprisonment.

Activity 38 · 5 mins

The Operations Director (OD) of a large company invested more than £1 million in new handling equipment at the end of a major production line. The intention was to save around 40 staff positions, producing extensive financial savings.

The equipment did not perform as claimed; no jobs were saved and whenever the new equipment came on line, waste levels increased between five and tenfold. Unsurprisingly, it was kept out of service most of the time, save when senior managers insisted on running further trials, usually for an eight-hour shift in response to the OD's direct orders.

The local staff (whom the intention was to make redundant) were appalled at the waste of a food product which the machine literally threw on the floor, and agreed a system amongst themselves.

■ The machine would be used only under direct instructions from the OD or the local General Manager (GM), who was always too busy to intervene.
■ When it was in use, there would be an emergency system to collect product from the conveyor, place it on trays and pack it during quiet periods later on. This involved the staff in frantic extra work, outside their normal job specification.

How would you have acted had you taken over this area from the existing manager? Would you have:

■ insisted that staff used the machinery at all times in accordance with the OD's wishes;
■ told them that their practice was against company rules and that waste levels were not their affair;
■ commended the team for their concern to save the company money;
■ taken up the machine's problems with the GM and your colleagues in the engineering function, making an unanswerable case to have it removed?

_____

_____

The chances are that you would have taken the third and fourth courses of action, which display common sense and proper financial and ethical concern for husbanding resources. But in doing so, you could have been accused of:

■ condoning a sub-culture of practices running contrary to that of the organization;
■ going outside the normal channels and becoming involved with internal politics that were none of your concern.

Activity 39

10 mins

Think about the culture – and possibly sub-cultures – in your organization.

■ What is your organization's preferred culture? Would you describe it as, for example:
　■ autocratic and given to 'shaming and blaming';
　■ paternalistic – that is, discouraging people from taking responsibility or showing initiative;
　■ empowering – that is, devolving authority wherever practicable and encouraging people to show initiative?

Describe the culture in your own words.

_____

_____

_____

■ Identify any sub-cultures that have developed that:
　■ tend to have beneficial effects for the organization as a whole;
　■ may have adverse effects on the organization as a whole.

What steps have you taken (or are taking) to encourage or eliminate them as appropriate?

_____

_____

_____

5 Internal politics

Two experienced managers were comparing their new general manager to his predecessor.

> 'With Joe Lyle,' said one, 'You never quite knew what was happening but you knew something was'.
> 'Aye,' replied the other, 'where with this one, if nothing seems to be happening, then nothing is happening'.

The difference between the two general managers was that the former one was a 'political animal' – good at getting things done, though not always through the proper channels.

In many ways, 'manager' and 'politician' are interchangeable words. Unfortunately, party politics throughout the world has coloured the word 'politician' with the image of self-serving characters, interested in no one's welfare but their own and indifferent as to whether anything gets done at all – provided they remain in office.

Not all politicians are corrupt and not all managers are virtuous. It is unlikely you will ever find an effective manager who does not practise some of the political arts instinctively. Internal politics, too, is often seen in an unflattering light, but frequently managers are using their initiative and determination to get things done, despite the defects in their organization's structure and culture.

5.1 Ambition and politics

No matter what the structure may be, there are fewer senior posts than there are managers wishing to fill them. So, ambitious managers try to ensure that they will be amongst the select few through demonstrated superior performance, or by gaining the support of those in whose gift the promotion lies.

Though performance may appear to be an objective way of establishing credentials for an ambitious manager, there are 'lies, damned lies and statistics'. Standards can be manipulated by less scrupulous managers. A particular interpretation or gloss can be put on the figures to suit a manager's personal aims and ambitions.

It is impossible to imagine human life without ambition. But many of the faults of politics are due to the ambitions of people who see no virtue in doing a job for its own sake. Rather, they see it as a stepping stone to another job – usually a more highly paid one.

5.2 Organizational structures and reporting relationships

You may find it helpful to look back at the charts in Session A while studying this section

Equivalent relationships exist in the military sphere. Many books, of fact and fiction, describe the rivalries, jealousy and sheer hatred which can arise between the line officers at the front and the general staff back at base. The lines of communication are similar – and so too are the chances for intrigue and politics. In civilian life, the issues are clouded further by the lack of any automatic respect for superior rank and seniority.

The structures and specialist functions described in Session A themselves create many possibilities for political manoeuvring.

Specialist managers, from production, marketing and other functions, will claim that their function is the most important and that its voice should be heard above all others. If their senior manager shares their background, there is a good chance that he or she **will** listen to a voice speaking a language which is familiar. Organizations are then often taken in the direction that a senior manager's **previous** experience has indicated was fruitful.

This is not surprising. People pursue a special discipline because they think it interesting and important – just as musicians take up the violin, or the trumpet, because they have an affinity with it above other instruments.

Political problems arise when there are eight or ten different specialists, who all believe that their voice should be heard above the others.

5.3 Line and staff relationships

The normal organization chart shows the 'line of command' passing from Company Managing Director to General Manager (GM) to Departmental Manager to First Line Manager to Operator. In principle;

- line managers have direct authority
- staff managers are limited to giving advice.

But frequently there are staff managers in specialist functions who report directly to the Managing Director (MD). The links between the line managers and specialists are usually known as 'staff' or 'dotted line' relationships, because of the way they are drawn on conventional charts.

Staff managers tend to have the ear of the 'MD' far more often than the General Manager of a remote site. They are frequently highly articulate specialists with a pride in their speciality as well as ambitions of their own. In practice, a staff manager who is theoretically less senior than a GM can exert influence far beyond what their official grade implies, and in extreme cases make it very difficult for a GM to exert real control over staff.

Functional management

If an organization adopts the functional management approach described in Session A, the reporting relationships become extremely complex. In extreme cases, the organization runs the risk of paralysis or chaos, with no one knowing who has authority to do anything.

5.4 Informal reporting relationships

Public limited companies (plcs) usually have 'non executive directors' who have no direct authority within the company. They are retained in an advisory role to provide expertise which might otherwise not be available. They do provide further lines of communication outside the formal management structure and their role is increasingly scrutinized.

In addition to the lines shown on the organization chart, there are frequently informal avenues of communication which don't appear. These avenues may be open for almost any reason, from membership of particular clubs, to friendships formed at school, to favours owed for services rendered perhaps many years ago.

A managing director may listen harder to the shop steward who once helped to avoid a disastrous strike than to the nominal deputy on the board. There also may be an 'elder statesman' figure in a family-run company, or a senior external adviser – a lawyer or accountant – or a major shareholder who needs to be asked.

The possible permutations are effectively infinite. Informal relationships are a fact of human life. Just about everyone has trusted friends and acquaintances, whose opinions they respect and whose goodwill they feel sure of. In organizations such friendships also provide opportunities for intrigue and for decisions to be taken outside the supposed chain of command.

Taken to extremes, they can undermine managers' authority completely and lead to illegal insider trading, where selected outsiders are given privileged information about movements in share prices.

Activity 40

5 mins

Think about your own experience of work and identify one or two situations in which you have gone outside the proper channels to make something positive happen that was in the interests of the organization for which you were working at the time.

Briefly describe the situations, then note down the informal communications channels you employed and whether they were within your organization, or with customers, suppliers or other organizations.

_____

_____

_____

_____

_____

There are, of course, numerous ways in which you might have responded to Activity 40. Here is just a sample of the sort of situations you might have described.

- Contacting a despatch department to persuade a colleague known to you that they should make a special effort **today** to help out a customer who has received the wrong order.
- Talking informally to a member of a customer's staff and persuading them to re-schedule an order so that you can avoid an expensive change within a long production run.
- Contacting someone you know in a bought ledger department to influence them to pay a company invoice on time.
- Persuading a supplier to make an order your company needs urgently 'out of sequence'.
- Persuading a haulier to take out a part-load, plainly not profitable in itself, in the interests of their long-term relationships with your organization.
- Influencing a shop steward or safety representative in your present or former union not to pursue an unreasonable grievance on behalf of an employee.

5.5 The manager as politician

EXTENSION 3
This contains some suggestions for further reading and other sources of information that will take you further into the world of organizations.

There are no answers to management issues that are right for all situations. Managers may engage in political manoeuvres out of motives covering a spectrum ranging from philanthropy to vaulting ambition. The same manager may exhibit a wide range of motivations at different times in their career.

As a manager you need to be aware of internal politics and how they arise. Certainly if you are ambitious and wish to get things done, you will need to acquire sufficient political skill to influence people – at least so that they will listen to what you have to say.

Communication is the most important part of the manager's job.

Internal politics are a vital aspect of communication in many organizations – for good or ill.

Effective managers must be able to use all the communication channels open to them – including the political ones when necessary.

Self-assessment 3

15 mins

1 Complete the following sentence.

Attempts to change the culture of an organization often _____

because change is _____ by _____ management rather

than _____ from the _____ up.

2 What do the letters MAS stand for and what does MAS attempt to measure?

_____

_____

3 List four phrases that describe different kinds of organizational culture.

_____

_____

_____

_____

4 Complete the following sentence.

In blame cultures within organizations, managers tend to become _____

looking and forget that _____ profit is generated inside a business,

only _____ .

5 Underline three examples of possible drawbacks to problem-solving cultures
from the following list:
a avoiding uncongenial tasks;
b losing focus on external threats;
c keeping detailed records of everything done;
d passing the buck;
e losing a sense of urgency

6 Re-arrange these words into a classic principle of management.

without never authority you responsibility delegate should

_____

7 Complete the following sentence.

For _____ organizations, the _____ are increasingly

looking to identify a _____ _____ who must take ultimate

_____ for its actions just as a _____ trader must.

8 Complete the following sentence by selecting words from this list.

transparency   rigidity   informality   autocracy   are   openness
are not   dictatorship   democracy

_____ is often confused with _____ and _____.

They _____ the same things

9 Give three reasons why internal politics arise in organizations.

_____

_____

_____

Answers to these questions can be found on pages 122–23.

6 Summary

- Organizations operating in the same sphere can appear very different to their staff, customers and clients because they have developed different cultures, with management styles and organizational structures to match them.

- The overall culture will normally stem from the top management's ethical stance, particularly when there is a dominant personality involved at the top.

- Cultures leaning towards assigning blame and a hire and fire mentality produce a defensive reaction in managers and staff, making them inward-looking and less focused on customers or clients who are the real reason for the organization's existence.

- Problem-solving cultures tend to promote initiative and integrity and create a much more fertile environment for teams and individuals to grow and become greater than the sum of their parts.

- Even in the most autocratic and punitive cultural systems, backed by threats and punishments, some specialists will need to be given licence to think outside the rigid reporting relationships imposed by the structure.

- Sub-cultures will develop, for benign or malign reasons, within many organizations. Senior management must be aware of them, in order to spread any good practices which flow from them and weed out those which run contrary to the organization's values and objectives.

- Difficulties arise for individuals when the organization's cultural values conflict with their own, a situation which may require one or the other to change – or to part company.

- In the long term, it is leadership and effective communications which will enable top management to achieve organizational objectives. This is especially true when managers are seeking to change deep-rooted cultures, one of the most difficult tasks to undertake in every aspect of life.

- Politics, with a large or a small 'p', and management are both more art than science and depend ultimately on persuasion rather than power, whatever the 'preferred' culture, management style and reporting relationships may be.

- Managers will often develop political skills and exercise influence through informal relationships which bypass the official channels indicated by organization charts.

- As with the development of sub-cultures, internal politics can arise from the best of motivations, where managers perceive that the organization is failing to meet its stated objectives through inappropriate or unwieldy organizational structures.

Performance checks

1 Quick quiz

Jot down the answers to the following questions on *Organizational Culture and Context.*

Question 1 List five types of organizations that remain, or had their origins in, the voluntary and self help sectors.

_____

_____

Question 2 People will often find their way around rigid organizational structures, from the best of intentions. Can you suggest some ways in which they do so?

_____

_____

_____

Question 3 Complete the following sentence with a suitable phrase selected from the list below.

It is unwise for any business to risk too much time and money in starting a

business venture in a market sector that has _____.

a high profit potential
b a low barrier to entry
c several organizations already operating in it
d strict legal requirements as to product safety

Question 4   One of the following documents sets out the way in which a limited company must manage its affairs between the board of directors and the shareholders. Which of the following is it:

a its mission statement;
b the Memorandum of Association;
c the Articles of Association?

_____

Question 5   Complete the following sentence.

Hierarchies with _____ tiers of _____ tend to be _____ to _____ to _____ circumstances and so may be too _____ in a _____ changing business environment, whereas 'wheel' organizations may place _____ _____ responsibility on a single _____ _____ .

Question 6   Complete the following sentence.

The _____ an organization's mission statement is, the less _____ is it likely to be at _____ its' core _____ .

Question 7   Complete the following sentence with words selected from the list below.

paybacks, ethical, longer, stance, socially, short-term

Though there may be _____ _____ costs associated with taking a _____ responsible _____ _____ , there can be commercial _____ in the _____ term.

Question 8   Explain in your own words Lord Denning's concept of the 'directing mind' in a large organization.

_____

_____

_____

Question 9   How is 'enlightened self interest' on the part of an individual or organization beneficial?

_____

_____

_____

Question 10   Complete the following sentence.

You will get a better impression of an organization's _____ stance by looking at what it _____ than by _____ its _____ statement, however _____ _____ it seems to be.

Question 11   Re-arrange the following words into a sentence describing a principle of modern management.

always to remains who can responsibility directors only authority managers with delegate

_____

_____ .

Question 12   Complete the following sentence with phrases selected from the list below.

Four features of 'problem-solving' cultures are that they encourage a _____ , _____

_____ and _____ .

good working atmosphere   honesty/integrity
meticulous record keeping   looking for scapegoats
passing the buck   initiative and reasonable risk-taking
focus on customers/clients

Question 13   Complete the following sentence.

Even in _____ organizational cultures, it is often necessary to _____ specialist _____ to 'think outside the box'.

Question 14   Put a tick against the correct option below.

Staff who are empowered by their managers are more likely to:

a take an interest in the organization and subscribe to its' declared culture and values ☐

b feel less concerned about preserving the organization's money and resources ☐

c take time off work for sickness or work related stress. ☐

Question 15   In what ways do the jobs of a manager and a politician resemble each other?

_____

_____

_____

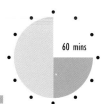

60 mins

2 Workbook assessment

Read through the case study below and imagine yourself as Hilary Arlington.

Hilary Arlington (HA) and two friends, Steve Newbury (SN) and Evelyn Hamilton (EH), had decided to set up their own business, running a high-street printing business. Hilary was a talented and experienced designer, Steve Newbury had an accounting background and worked for the Company Secretary of a plc, and Evelyn Hamilton had sales experience both 'on the road' as a sales manager and running a retail shop. They were sure that there was a substantial local market and as yet there was no competition. Hilary was the driving force behind the idea – the one to whom the others looked for general leadership and ideas. They estimated six full-time and part-time staff would be needed.

A meeting was arranged to discuss the many decisions that had to be taken before they left their present jobs. Ahead of the meeting, Hilary set down the organizational options as they appeared and formulated some recommendations for the others.

The options as Hilary saw them are shown on page 109.

Decision required	OPTION 1	OPTION 2	OPTION 3	OPTION 4
1 Legal structure (choose one option)	partnership	private limited company	public limited company (plc)	franchise from national operator
2 Assignment of responsibility (select one option from every box)	General direction/design/ production/quality HA/SN/EH	Marketing/sales/ product development HA/SN/EH	Finance/ Accounting HA/SN/EH	Personnel/payroll HA/SN/EH
3 External finance/support (select up to 3)	None	family members/ friends	Bank/finance company	franchise company
4 Stakeholders (choose one option only)	HA/SN/EH	HA/SN/EH + capital providers	HA/SN/EH + capital providers + customers	HA/SN/EH + capital providers + customers + employees
5 Ethical stance (choose one option only)	None (save minimum legal obligations)	Equal opportunities employer (EOE)	EOE + Environmentally aware (EA)	EOE + EA + social obligations
6 Mission statement (choose one option only)	None	"To provide top quality at lowest prices"	"Quality, Service' Value for money"	"Service to all, large or small"
7 Organizational culture & management style (one choice only)	Autocratic – Hilary as central decision taker for all major decisions	All decisions agreed by HA/ SN/EH	Problem solving – with involvement of all staff through hierarchy	Empowering – delegating all decisions to most effective level

Decide which options you would choose, **were you in Hilary's position**, observing the guidelines given for how many choices to make against each decision. Then, in the table that follows, give a **brief** rationale for the decisions you have taken.

Bear in mind that this is a new business and may require a different initial approach from that which you would advocate for a mature one.

Decision	Rationale for options selected
1 Legal structure	
2 Assignment of responsibility	
3 External finance/ support	
4 Stakeholders	
5 Ethical stance	
6 Mission statement	
7 Organizational culture & management style	

The issues you have considered on behalf of Hilary and friends are faced by every business, new or old, of any size, whatever they do. From local shops to multinational conglomerates, all must decide on these matters or see them go 'by default', in which case they will be storing up trouble at some time in the future.

3 Work-based assignment

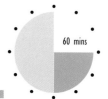

60 mins

S/NVQ C4.2, C4.3

The time guide for this assignment gives you an approximate idea of how long it is likely to take you to write up your findings. You will find you need to spend some additional time gathering information, perhaps talking to colleagues and thinking about the assignment.

Your written response to this assignment could form the basis of useful evidence for your S/NVQ portfolio. This workbook provides you with an understanding of the factors that shape the way organizations operate. It helps to develop your competence across a wide range of elements of the

Management Standards used in S/NVQs in Management. It is particularly relevant to developing your competence in:

- behaving ethically;
- managing self.

In the three sessions of this workbook you have looked at:

a the reasons for having organizations and some of the forms they can take;

b the ethics of organizations and the differing stances they take to a range of issues;

c the varying cultures, sub-cultures and internal politics of organizations.

In this assignment, you are asked to research and describe aspects (b) and (c) of your own organization, or one that you previously worked for or are familiar with outside work. Incorporate existing documentation wherever appropriate.

Business ethics

List the ethical values of the organization you have chosen:

- as they are stated in documents such as mission statements, annual reports, newsletters, team briefing documents or on notice boards;
- as expressed in other ways, such as press releases or statements to the national or local media; participation in national or local schemes; supporting charitable and community or environmental issues.

Describe the organization's ethics as you perceive them in action, for example, in the way the organization deals with customers, suppliers, employees, former employees and the local or wider community. Look particularly at any stakeholders identified in the documentation you have read through.

Organizational culture

For the organization you have selected:

- describe the dominant culture it exhibits, giving examples of the management styles that have developed to support it;
- outline any sub-cultures of which you are aware in the organization as a whole or in your own area, saying whether you believe they are helpful or unhelpful in achieving the organization's overall goals;
- describe any internal politics that affect you, for good or otherwise, where people act outside the formal structure and reporting relationships.

Reflect and review

1 Reflect and review

This is an appropriate time to review the objectives set for *Organizational Culture and Context*.

When you have completed this workbook, you will be better able to do the following.

■ Understand the value of an organization to achieving objectives and the power of an organization to act by comparison with non-organized action.

Are you now clear about the true worth of an organization in achieving a stated purpose and objectives, as contrasted with a group of individuals without an agreed purpose, organizational structure and means of co-ordinating their activities, even though they may all individually wish to act in the same way?

■ Describe the forms that organizations can take, the functions required to maintain them and the proper roles of managers at various levels within them.

Do you now have a clear picture of the various forms of organization, and the advantages and drawbacks each form may have? Are you clear about the support that they need from specialist functions, and the true role of managers in supporting, rather than bearing down upon, their staff? Can you relate the principles to your own organization and immediate situation?

■ Distinguish between different organizational structures and their 'fitness for purpose' in differing situations.

Can you now recognize different structures and the organizational purposes that they will help achieve? Is it clear that there is no one structure which will serve all purposes, and that the structure must match the purpose of the organization? Does the structure of your own employer's organization match the purposes that it is supposed to help achieve?

■ Recognise the importance of organizational and business ethics in general and their application to your own workplace.

You should now have a clearer idea of the different positions that organizations may take over ethical questions and where your own fits into the spectrum.

■ Understand the concept of stakeholders and identify the stakeholders in your organization.

The various groups who can genuinely claim to have a stake in the continuing prosperity of an organization should be apparent to you, both in general terms and in relation to your own organization.

■ Appreciate the conflicts that can exist between individuals' values and those of the organization for which they work .

The frictions that can exist when there is little or no synergy between what an individual values and what an organization values have been examined from various perspectives. You should have a clearer idea of what organizational values will 'fit' with your own.

■ Understand the range of organizational cultures that may exist and recognize their specific effect on your own workplace.

You should be able to identify the effects of different cultural stances emanating from top management and/or long-established custom and practice in your own working experience. The development of sub-cultures, which may have good or bad effects, have also been described and again you should be able to relate the principles to your own working experience.

■ Recognize the value of delegated authority and be ready to use it within your own working environment.

The positive effects of empowering people by delegating defined limits of authority have been illustrated. The fact that authority can be delegated, but that ultimate responsibility always remains with an organization's senior management, has also been underlined, for you to test against your own experience.

2 Action plan

Use this plan to further develop for yourself a course of action you want to take. Make a note in the left-hand column of the issues or problems you want to tackle, and then decide what you want to do, and make a note in column 2.

The resources you need might include time, materials, information or money. You may need to negotiate for some of them, but they could be something easily acquired, like half an hour of somebody's time, or a chapter of a book. Put whatever you need in column 3. No plan means anything without a timescale, so put a realistic target completion date in column 4.

Finally, describe the outcome you want to achieve as a result of this plan, whether it is for your own benefit or advancement, or a more efficient way of doing things.

Desired outcomes				
1 Issues	2 Action	3 Resources	4 Target completion
Actual outcomes				

3 Extensions

Extension 1

Two well organized systems which affect the daily lives of everyone reading this book are:

- computer software;
- the human internal organization.

Computer software

This workbook is being written though a computer-based word processor's software, one of a number of such systems on which the whole publication process from this point forward depends. Into this system is built file handling arrangements, routines for organizing the text into the desired format, including font sizes, spacing, **emboldening**, *italicising* and under-lining words, indenting or numbering systems and putting text into tabular form to facilitate editing by the author.

The functions provided are so numerous that it would be too time-consuming to list them here. In addition, there are numerous commands available which the computer is organized to respond to instantly – including spell checking, counting the words written, saving the data into the core memory or to disk, previewing text to be printed.

The software is organized to provide communication to a colour printer (a complex piece of organization in itself) or to remote locations via fax or email, all at the touch of a button or use of the ingenious mouse system.

- The author can take all these facilities for granted, provided that the people who designed the software systems – and organized all its operational functions – did so in a way which will achieve the purpose that the computer is intended to serve.
- He or she needs to know nothing about how and why the facilities work - they simply get on with it amongst the electronic devices which the click of a mouse, or touch of a key, activates.

The human internal organization

Likewise, the author does not need to keep examining, still less tinkering, with the internal human organization that has evolved over countless ages and works for the most part extremely well. The organs that function to extract useable components from food, circulate it to all those functions which need it and to repel assaults by unwelcome micro organisms are organized to carry on functioning over many years without making their presence known.

Both organizations, the one designed and developed over several decades by humans and the other resulting from subtle evolutionary changes over countless centuries, illustrate how the best organizations are virtually invisible. They truly run on 'oiled wheels' so far as the casual observer is concerned – and that is what is desired of **any** effective organization.

Extension 2

MISSION STATEMENT
ALPHA & OMEGA plc
Always first and built to last

This Company intends to use world-class manufacturing and management practices to assure the best interests of all the recognised stakeholders in our business: customers, employees and former employees, suppliers, the local community and the wider environment.

About customers

We are determined to exceed our customers' expectations of us regarding products and services at all times. In our business, the customer is truly the king.

About employees

Employees are our most valuable resource. We will ensure that all our employees achieve contentment in their work and do not regard any as just 'another employee'. If an employee has a problem, then it is as much our problem than his or hers. We will continue our concern for welfare through into the retirement years of our former employees.

About suppliers

We believe in promoting partnership with our suppliers and developing long-term relationships with them to the mutual benefit of both parties. This we extend to overseas suppliers in countries where our business is vital to the local economy.

About our neighbours and the environment

We have regard always to the potential impact of our activities on the local community and the wider environment and use every endeavour to eliminate any adverse effects that we might produce in either.

Graham Bowmond, Chief Executive Officer

Extension 3   Further reading and listening

Organizations, what they do and how they do it are the subject of countless textbooks and vast numbers of novels. It is a topic concerning which the novelist can often reveal insights into the minds of the characters playing out the story.

Because the law changes and approaches to organizational management change, it is also very helpful to listen to the radio and read the broadsheet press to keep up-to-date.

1 Non fiction

Book   *Understanding Organizations*
Author   Charles Handy
Edition   4th February 1993, ISBN 0140156038
Pubisher   Penguin

Charles Handy is an authority on the subject and writes in an attractive, readable style. He argues, in this classic work, that the key to successful organizations lies in a better understanding of the needs and motivations of the people within them, whether they be schools, hospitals, charities, or commercial companies.

Book   *The Prince*
Author   Niccolo Machiavelli
Edition   1993, ISBN 1–85326–306–0
Pubisher   Wordsworth Reference

This book is a series of short, readable essays on aspects of leadership, government and politics. The fact that it is still in print almost 500 years after the essays were written shows how well Machiavelli grasped his subject. The fact that his thoughts are still relevant shows how little human nature has changed.

2 Fiction

There are thousands of novels on these topics, of which you may have read many. Some following titles are specific recommendations which are relevant to this workbook.

Book   *The Corridors of Power*
Author   C.P. Snow

Snow was a scientist who worked as an adviser to governments and knew politics from the inside. This, the best known in his series of political novels, gives an insider's view on the priorities of politicians and their way of getting things done through the political channels open to them.

Book   *The Way We Live Now*
Author   Anthony Trollope

As well as being a distinguished novelist, Trollope was one of the instigators (in the 1840s) of the universal single rate postal system still enjoyed in the UK more than 150 years later. He understood politics, organizations and business very well and this book in particular has never lost its relevance to the way that 'big business' may operate.

3 Newspapers

Most of the broadsheet daily and Sunday newspapers, national and regional, carry business and financial news, well-presented and often well-illustrated to explain complex topics. The reporters and editors are experts in their fields, well-briefed and reasonably free of political bias towards one party or another.

Reading any from the following list (most of which will appear in local libraries as well as on the news stands) would help to keep you up-to-date and build on the foundations provided by this book.

The Financial Times	The Times	The Daily Telegraph
The Guardian	The Independent	The Observer
The Scotsman	The Aberdeen Press & Journal	The Yorkshire Post
The Sunday Times	The Cardiff Western Mail	The Sunday Telegraph
	The Independent on Sunday	

4 Radio and Television

BBC Radio 4 in particular provides both news and in-depth coverage of issues covered by this book. TV news, including the early evening Channel 4 bulletin, also cover such issues, but not usually in great depth. Schedules are published in newspapers, the Radio Times and on teletext and equivalents.

4 Answers to self-assessment questions

**Self-assessment 1
on pages 40–1**

1 The sign of a **good/well run** organization is that the **whole** is **greater** than the sum of its parts.

2 **Excellent management communications** is the basis for continuing success in any successful organization in the long term.

3 Investing in a company's shares removes from investors the threat of **unlimited personal liability**.

4 Among the disadvantages that partnerships share with sole traders are unlimited personal liability; difficulty in raising substantial sums of money; difficulty in organizing succession as original personnel changes.

5 Becoming a franchisee is now popular as a way of starting, or expanding, a business because it provides a private individual, or fairly small organization, with the marketing 'clout' of a powerful brand – **provided** they choose the right franchising organization.

6 The two kinds of limited liability company are Private Limited and Public Limited Companies. The latter is often abbreviated to 'plc' and can, unlike a 'private' company, sell its shares to unlimited numbers of shareholders via the stock exchange.

7 Neither limited companies, nor registered charities, can do anything legally other than what is covered by the objectives that they state when they register.

8 One of the principal differences between a public sector and a private sector organization is that the former is a **cost centre** whereas the latter is a **profit centre.**

9 When considering a major **reorganization** of their **activity**, senior managers should bear in mind the maxim 'that no **profit** is generated inside a **business**, only **cost**'.

**Self-assessment 2
on pages 69–70**

1 Four potential groups of stakeholders in an organization are **shareholders, customers, employees, suppliers, the local community, neighbours** (choose any from this list).

2 **Objective** judgements are based on **facts** whereas **value** judgements are based on **opinions**.

3 In broad terms, you will probably have disagreed with the statement. The situation which it describes should lead to **synergy** between the individual and the organization.

4 There are many examples of organizations which have combined a sense of **social** responsibility with **long-**term commercial **success.**

5 You probably said something along the lines that it's very easy to criticize others for poor ethical standards when you do not have the responsibility for taking the difficult decisions that they face.

6 Public relations briefings are **a professional** way of communicating the organization's values to the wider world. You may have selected another phrase, depending on the value judgement which you have formed about public relations.

7 The 'Whistleblowing Act' is a nickname for the Public Interest Disclosure Act (PIDA). It is dealt with by the Employment Tribunals.

8 Matters such as breaches of the law, health & safety, breaches of contract, and the environment can all be 'protected disclosures' under PIDA.

Self-assessment 3 on pages 101–2

1 Attempts to change the culture of an organization often **fail** because change is **imposed** by **senior/top** management rather than **grown/nurtured** from the **bottom/grass roots** up.

2 MAS is an abbreviation for Management Attitude Survey. A MAS attempts to measure the views of managers on the culture of the organization for which they work by means of a confidential survey.

3 Words or phrases which describe different kinds of organizational culture could include:

■ paternalistic;
■ autocratic;
■ hire and fire;
■ problem solving.

4 In blame cultures within organizations, managers tend to become **inward** looking and forget that **no** profit is generated inside a business, only **cost**.

5 Possible drawbacks to problem-solving cultures from the following list are:

a avoiding uncongenial tasks;
b losing focus on external threats;
c losing a sense of urgency.

6   You should never delegate responsibility without authority.

7   For **large** organizations, the **courts/law-makers** are increasingly looking to identify a **directing mind** who must take ultimate **responsibility** for its actions just as a **sole** trader must.

8   **Informality** is often confused with **openness** and **transparency**. They **are not** the same things.

9   Internal politics arise in organizations for many reasons including:

   ■ ambitions of managers;
   ■ informal and 'dotted line' reporting relationships;
   ■ failure by senior management to convince staff of the 'rightness' of the organizational culture.

5 Answers to activities

Activity 5 on page 9

Sole traders can be involved with almost anything, including:

■ trades – window cleaning; chimney sweeping; car maintenance; running almost every kind of retailing (including market stalls, shops; mobile shops); gardening; tree surgery; building trades (plumbing; bricklaying; carpentry/ joinery; glazing) ; courier services; agricultural contracting;

■ professions: accountancy, the law; writing; editing; acting; individual sports (including tennis, squash, golf); medicine and veterinary services; management consultancy; financial services; property services; auctioneering.

Your list probably contained some of these ways of earning a living but may well have included many others.

Activity 10 on pages 21–2

The rewritten sentence should read:
'The purpose of this Company is to manufacture, distribute and sell **any** form of **transportation** for use by individuals or public service operators.'

This gives the company the flexibility it needs to respond to changes in the market.

Reflect and review

Activity 11 on page 23	Public sector organizations include the following. ■ Hospitals, NHS medical and dentistry services ■ Schools, colleges & universities ■ Royal Mail ■ Government departments – Inland Revenue, Customs & Excise, Social Security ■ Police, ambulance service and fire brigades ■ The Environment Agency ■ Trading standards and regulatory bodies like the Financial Services Authority ■ The armed forces and intelligence/anti espionage services
Activity 13 on pages 25–6	Many organizations sprang from poverty and inequality between employers and employees in nineteenth-century Britain and continue to function in the twenty first century. They include the following. ■ Trades Unions. ■ Co-operative Societies. ■ Building Societies. ■ Friendly Societies. ■ Mutual Societies.
Activity 19 on pages 39–40	The specialist functions which a modern organization is likely to have are as follows. 1 Finance 2 Marketing/product development 3 Sales 4 Distribution 5 Human resources 6 Production 7 Engineering/Technical 8 Public relations 9 Research 10 Information technology 11 Safety/Environment/Risk management No order of priority is implied by the list. The names of departments and the mix will vary according to the purpose of the organization.
Activity 20 on page 44	The following solution is provided for you to compare your own selections and priority order with, but there is no (2+2) = 4 solution which works for all situations and organizations. This suggestion assumes that the organization is already fulfilling its' legal obligations.

Young people (0)	**General public (8)**	Wildlife (0)
Shareholders (2)	**Employees (3)**	**Creditors (6)**
Company pensioners (4)	Charity (0)	**Neighbours (7)**
Disadvantaged groups (0)	**Customers (1)**	**Environment (9)**
Local community (10)	**Suppliers (5)**	Education/Training (0)

Activity 23 on page 49

Statements 1, 4, 5 and 6 are value judgements, which there is no numerical way of testing. Statements 2, 3 and 7 are matters of historical fact.

Activity 30 on pages 76–7

Situation 1	gradualist	benign	team-centred
Situation 2	swashbuckling go-getting	task-centred adventurous	individualistic
Situation 3	paternalistic	benign	cautious

Activity 31 on pages 79–80

Some suggestions as to what would be helpful or not from the twelve options given are as follows.

1 helpful	2 neutral	3 unhelpful	4 very unhelpful
5 neutral	6 helpful	7 very unhelpful	8 helpful
9 very unhelpful	10 unhelpful	11 neutral	12 very helpful

6 Answers to the quick quiz

Answer 1 You might have listed any of the following: Charities; Trades Unions; Mutual and Friendly societies; Building Societies; Co-operative societies; Workers' education societies; Credit Unions; Professional associations and Craft Guilds, amongst others known to you.

Answer 2 People often find their way around rigid organizational structures by using initiative, acting speedily before the organization can find out what they are doing, and by developing their political skills to use unofficial communication channels.

Answer 3   It is unwise for any business to risk too much time and money in starting a business venture in a market sector that has **a low barrier to entry**.

Answer 4   **The Articles of Association** set out the way in which a limited company must manage its affairs as between the board of directors and the shareholders.

Answer 5   Hierarchies with **many** tiers of **management** tend to be **slow** to **react** to **changing** circumstances and so may be too **inflexible** in a **rapidly** changing business environment, whereas 'wheel' organizations may place **too much** responsibility on a single **senior manager/decision-taker**.

Answer 6   The **longer/more detailed** an organization's mission statement is, the less **useful/helpful** is it likely to be at **communicating** its core **values**.

Answer 7   Though there may be **short-term** costs associated with taking a **socially** responsible **ethical stance**, there can be commercial **paybacks** in the **longer** term.

Answer 8   Lord Denning's concept of the 'directing mind' makes it increasingly difficult for senior managers and the chief executive to hide behind layers of management and complex organizational structures.

Answer 9   'Enlightened self interest' is beneficial in that it creates a situation where both parties to a transaction can take something positive from it, including in the medium to long term.

Answer 10   You will get a better impression of an organization's **ethical** stance by looking at what it **does** than by **reading** its **mission** statement, however **well-intentioned** it seems to be.

Answer 11   Responsibility always remains with directors who can only delegate authority to managers.

Answer 12   Four features of problem-solving cultures are that they encourage a **good working atmosphere, a focus on customers/clients, honesty/integrity**, and **initiative/reasonable risk-taking**.

Answer 13   Even in **autocratic/dictatorial** organizational cultures, it is often necessary to **permit/allow** specialist **managers** to 'think outside the box'.

Answer 14   Staff who are empowered by their managers are more likely to (a) take an interest in the organization and subscribe to its' declared culture and values.

Answer 15   The jobs of managers and politicians resemble each other **in that both have to achieve results through other people, most often through persuasion rather than force.**

7 Certificate

Completion of the certificate by an authorized person shows that you have worked through all the parts of this workbook and satisfactorily completed the assessments. The certificate provides a record of what you have done that may be used for exemptions or as evidence of prior learning against other nationally certificated qualifications.

Pergamon Flexible Learning and ILM are always keen to refine and improve their products. One of the key sources of information to help this process is people who have just used the product. If you have any information or views, good or bad, please pass these on.

INSTITUTE OF LEADERSHIP & MANAGEMENT

SUPERSERIES

Organizational Culture and Context

....

has satisfactorily completed this workbook

Name of signatory ....

Position ....

Signature ....

Date ....

Official stamp

Fourth Edition

INSTITUTE OF LEADERSHIP & MANAGEMENT
SUPERSERIES
FOURTH EDITION

To order – phone us direct for prices and availability details
(please quote ISBNs when ordering) on 01865 888190